INDICATORS OF EDUCATION SYSTEMS

INDICATEURS DES S
D'ENSEIGNEM

# EDUCATION
# AND EMPLOYMENT

# FORMATION
# ET EMPLOI

ORGANISATION FOR ECONOMIC CO-OPERATION AND DEVELOPMENT
ORGANISATION DE COOPÉRATION ET DE DÉVELOPPEMENT ÉCONOMIQUES

# ORGANISATION FOR ECONOMIC CO-OPERATION AND DEVELOPMENT

Pursuant to Article 1 of the Convention signed in Paris on 14th December 1960, and which came into force on 30th September 1961, the Organisation for Economic Co-operation and Development (OECD) shall promote policies designed:

— to achieve the highest sustainable economic growth and employment and a rising standard of living in Member countries, while maintaining financial stability, and thus to contribute to the development of the world economy;

— to contribute to sound economic expansion in Member as well as non-member countries in the process of economic development; and

— to contribute to the expansion of world trade on a multilateral, non-discriminatory basis in accordance with international obligations.

The original Member countries of the OECD are Austria, Belgium, Canada, Denmark, France, Germany, Greece, Iceland, Ireland, Italy, Luxembourg, the Netherlands, Norway, Portugal, Spain, Sweden, Switzerland, Turkey, the United Kingdom and the United States. The following countries became Members subsequently through accession at the dates indicated hereafter: Japan (28th April 1964), Finland (28th January 1969), Australia (7th June 1971), New Zealand (29th May 1973) and Mexico (18th May 1994). The Commission of the European Communities takes part in the work of the OECD (Article 13 of the OECD Convention).

*The Centre for Educational Research and Innovation was created in June 1968 by the Council of the Organisation for Economic Co-operation and Development and all Member countries of the OECD are participants.*

*The main objectives of the Centre are as follows:*

— *to promote and support the development of research activities in education and undertake such research activities where appropriate;*

— *to promote and support pilot experiments with a view to introducing and testing innovations in the educational system;*

— *to promote the development of co-operation between Member countries in the field of educational research and innovation.*

*The Centre functions within the Organisation for Economic Co-operation and Development in accordance with the decisions of the Council of the Organisation, under the authority of the Secretary-General. It is supervised by a Governing Board composed of one national expert in its field of competence from each of the countries participating in its programme of work.*

# ORGANISATION DE COOPÉRATION
# ET DE DÉVELOPPEMENT ÉCONOMIQUES

En vertu de l'article 1er de la Convention signée le 14 décembre 1960, à Paris, et entrée en vigueur le 30 septembre 1961, l'Organisation de Coopération et de Développement Économiques (OCDE) a pour objectif de promouvoir des politiques visant :

— à réaliser la plus forte expansion de l'économie et de l'emploi et une progression du niveau de vie dans les pays Membres, tout en maintenant la stabilité financière, et à contribuer ainsi au développement de l'économie mondiale ;

— à contribuer à une saine expansion économique dans les pays Membres, ainsi que les pays non membres, en voie de développement économique ;

— à contribuer à l'expansion du commerce mondial sur une base multilatérale et non discriminatoire conformément aux obligations internationales.

Les pays Membres originaires de l'OCDE sont : l'Allemagne, l'Autriche, la Belgique, le Canada, le Danemark, l'Espagne, les États-Unis, la France, la Grèce, l'Irlande, l'Islande, l'Italie, le Luxembourg, la Norvège, les Pays-Bas, le Portugal, le Royaume-Uni, la Suède, la Suisse et la Turquie. Les pays suivants sont ultérieurement devenus Membres par adhésion aux dates indiquées ci-après : le Japon (28 avril 1964), la Finlande (28 janvier 1969), l'Australie (7 juin 1971), la Nouvelle-Zélande (29 mai 1973) et le Mexique (18 mai 1994). La Commission des Communautés européennes participe aux travaux de l'OCDE (article 13 de la Convention de l'OCDE).

*Le Centre pour la Recherche et l'Innovation dans l'Enseignement a été créé par le Conseil de l'Organisation de Coopération et de Développement Économiques en juin 1968 et tous les pays Membres de l'OCDE y participent.*

*Les principaux objectifs du Centre sont les suivants :*

— *encourager et soutenir le développement des activités de recherche se rapportant à l'éducation et entreprendre, le cas échéant, des activités de cette nature ;*

— *encourager et soutenir des expériences pilotes en vue d'introduire des innovations dans l'enseignement et d'en faire l'essai ;*

— *encourager le développement de la coopération entre les pays Membres dans le domaine de la recherche et de l'innovation dans l'enseignement.*

*Le Centre exerce son activité au sein de l'Organisation de Coopération et de Développement Économiques conformément aux décisions du Conseil de l'Organisation, sous l'autorité du Secrétaire général et le contrôle direct d'un Comité directeur composé d'experts nationaux dans le domaine de compétence du Centre, chaque pays participant étant représenté par un expert.*

# Foreword

The General Assembly of the OECD project on International Indicators of Education Systems (INES) met in Lugano, Switzerland, in September 1991. That assembly reviewed the first set of OECD education indicators, and recommended that they be published in *Education at a Glance: OECD Indicators*. After the decision by the CERI Governing Board and the Education Committee in early 1992 to continue to develop education indicators, four networks with voluntary country participation were invited to pursue the conceptual and methodological work needed for the measurement of new indicators in different domains:

- Network A, led by the United States, took up the challenge of developing and measuring indicators of student learning outcomes;
- Network B, with strong support from Sweden, was requested to develop measures of education and labour market destinations;
- Network C, under the leadership of the Netherlands, was given the task of measuring indicators of schools and school processes;
- Network D, supported by the United Kingdom, was invited to chart the expectations and attitudes to education of the various stakeholder groups in OECD societies.

The General Assembly will convene again in June 1995, when Member countries and the people involved in the INES project will take stock of what has been achieved, examine the organisational framework of the sets of indicators produced so far, and explore the possibilities for further developments. To facilitate this review, each network has prepared a report describing the conceptual, methodological, and policy problems encountered in constructing its respective clusters of indicators. The four reports are presented to the INES General Assembly as background and reference documents. Collectively, they offer a rich account of innovations, successes and failures in indicator development at the OECD, information that is essential for a review of perspectives and options for possible future work.

The content of each report has been discussed and endorsed during plenary sessions of the networks. The contributors are mostly members and national delegates to the networks, although in some cases distinguished independent experts have also contributed. For each network, members reviewed all the papers and suggested modifications where needed.

The preparation of this report was made possible thanks to generous contributions and support received from Sweden, the lead country of Network B. This volume was prepared by the Network Chair, Bertil Bucht of the Swedish Ministry of Education and Science, and Kjell Härnqvist of the University of Göteborg, in co-operation with Norberto Bottani and Albert Tuijnman of the OECD Secretariat.

This report is published on the responsibility of the Secretary-General of the OECD. It represents the views of the authors and does not necessarily reflect those of the OECD or of its Member countries.

# Avant-propos

L'Assemblée générale du projet de l'OCDE sur les indicateurs internationaux des systèmes d'enseignement (INES) s'est réunie à Lugano, en Suisse, en septembre 1991. Elle a passé en revue la première série d'indicateurs de l'enseignement de l'OCDE et recommandé qu'ils soient publiés dans *Regards sur l'éducation : les indicateurs de l'OCDE.* Après que le Comité directeur du CERI et le Comité de l'éducation eurent décidé au début de 1992 de poursuivre l'élaboration d'indicateurs de l'enseignement, quatre réseaux, auxquels les pays participent volontairement, ont été invités à effectuer les travaux conceptuels et méthodologiques nécessaires pour mesurer de nouveaux indicateurs dans différents domaines :

- le Réseau A, mené par les États-Unis, s'est donné pour mission d'élaborer et de mesurer des indicateurs des acquis des élèves et étudiants ;
- le Réseau B, qui bénéficie d'une importante aide de la Suède, a été invité à mettre au point des mesures relatives à l'enseignement et aux débouchés professionnels ;
- le Réseau C, dirigé par les Pays-Bas, s'est vu confier la tâche de mesurer les indicateurs des établissements et des processus scolaires ;
- le Réseau D, soutenu par le Royaume-Uni, a été invité à décrire les attentes et les attitudes à l'égard de l'enseignement des diverses parties prenantes dans les pays de l'OCDE.

L'Assemblée générale se réunira de nouveau en juin 1995 ce qui permettra aux pays Membres et aux personnes participant au projet INES de faire le bilan de ce qui a été accompli, d'examiner l'organisation des séries d'indicateurs élaborés jusqu'à présent, et d'étudier les prolongements possibles. Pour faciliter cet examen, chaque réseau décrit dans un rapport les problèmes conceptuels, méthodologiques et politiques auxquels il s'est heurté dans la construction de sa propre série d'indicateurs. Les quatre rapports sont présentés à l'Assemblée générale du projet INES à titre de documents de référence. Ensemble, ils rendent compte en détail des innovations introduites avec ou sans succès dans la construction d'indicateurs à l'OCDE, autant d'informations qui sont essentielles pour étudier les perspectives et les options qui s'offrent en vue de la poursuite des travaux.

Le contenu de chaque rapport a été examiné et approuvé au cours des sessions plénières des réseaux. Les auteurs sont dans leur majorité des membres des réseaux et des personnes déléguées près d'eux par les pays, encore que dans certains cas des experts indépendants de haut niveau aient aussi apporté leur concours. Pour chacun des réseaux, les membres ont passé en revue tous les rapports et, le cas échéant, suggéré des modifications.

Ce rapport a été élaboré grâce à l'aide reçue de la Suède qui a assuré la direction du Réseau B, a généreusement contribué à sa publication et en a assuré la coordination. Cet ouvrage a été établi par le président du réseau, Bertil Bucht, du ministère suédois de l'Éducation et de la Science, et Kjell Härnqvist de l'Université de Göteborg, en coopération avec Norberto Bottani et Albert Tuijnman du Secrétariat de l'OCDE.

Ce rapport est publié sous la responsabilité du Secrétaire général de l'OCDE. Il reflète les opinions des auteurs et ne représente pas nécessairement le point de vue de l'OCDE ni celui de ses pays Membres.

# Table of Contents/Table des matières

*Chapter/Chapitre 1*

**Introduction**

*Bertil Bucht*

*Chapter/Chapitre 2*

**Indicators of Network B**
**Indicateurs du Réseau B**

*Olof Jos and Kenny Petersson*

9

*Chapter/Chapitre 3*

**Concepts and Definitions**
*Concepts et définitions*

*Thomas J. Healy and Allan Nordin*

*Chapter/Chapitre 4*

**Contextual Factors Surrounding Transitions from Education to the Labour Market**
*Facteurs contextuels influant sur le passage de la formation à la vie active*

*Kenneth D. Bennett*

*Chapter/Chapitre 8*

**Gender Disparities in Labour Market Outcomes of Education**
*Différences dans la situation des hommes et des femmes sur le marché du travail
à l'issue de leur formation*

*Nicholas Pole*

*Chapter/Chapitre 9*

**Methodological Issues in the Calculation of an Index of Gender Differences**
*Problèmes méthodologiques posés par le calcul d'un indice des disparités
entre les hommes et les femmes*

*Luc Van de Poele*

12

13

# Introduction

*by*

**Bertil Bucht**
Ministry of Education and Science, Stockholm, Sweden

This chapter describes the rationale for Network B. The main purpose of the Network B indicators is to provide tools for measuring the results of education and revealing problems in labour supply and demand. The network's background, domain of study and actual work are described. A highly relevant aspect in the domain of study of Network B is the transition from school to work and how different measures can promote this process. Another relevant aspect is the frequency of participation in continuing education and training among the labour force and the general adult population, and the amount of education and training received. In order to describe the economic outcomes of education, an indicator has been developed relating earnings from work to level of education. The final section offers an overview of the contents of this volume.

*

*     *

## Note de synthèse

*Ce chapitre décrit les objectifs et le programme de travail du Réseau B du projet de l'OCDE relatif aux indicateurs internationaux des systèmes d'enseignement (INES). Depuis 1990, une vingtaine de pays ont pris spontanément une part active à ce réseau qui a élaboré des indicateurs touchant l'enseignement et le marché du travail. Ce premier chapitre sert de toile de fond aux chapitres suivants en présentant la genèse et le programme d'activité effectif du réseau.*

*L'auteur indique plusieurs raisons pour lesquelles les pays ont porté autant d'intérêt à la mise au point d'indicateurs dans ce domaine. Certains pays ont souligné les effets de l'enseignement sur les débouchés professionnels, la productivité et la croissance économique. D'autres ont mis l'accent sur les coûts de l'enseignement, en faisant valoir qu'étant donné le niveau élevé des dépenses publiques et privées consacrées à l'enseignement et à la formation, il était impératif d'élaborer des indicateurs des résultats de l'enseignement, en particulier sur le marché du travail. Les pays Membres de l'OCDE se sont aussi, dans l'ensemble, déclarés préoccupés par les conséquences de la mondialisation pour leur compétitivité et se sont interrogés sur les investissements en capital humain et sur les conditions propices à un rendement optimal de ces investissements.*

*La principale raison d'être des indicateurs mis au point par le Réseau B du projet INES est de permettre de mesurer les résultats de l'enseignement en termes d'offre et de demande de main-d'œuvre. On peut, par exemple, mesurer l'emploi, le chômage et le niveau de formation de la population active. Un aspect très important du champ d'étude du Réseau B est le passage de l'école à la vie active ; il convient, en effet, de savoir comment différentes mesures peuvent faciliter ce processus de transition. C'est là une question politique et sociale capitale pour de nombreux pays Membres de l'OCDE. Un autre aspect qui mérite de retenir l'attention est la fréquence de la participation à la formation continue chez les actifs et les adultes en général. Pour décrire les résultats de l'enseignement sur le plan économique, on a mis au point un indicateur qui établit un lien entre le salaire et le niveau de formation. Cet indicateur du rendement de l'investissement consacré par l'individu à sa formation demande à être complété par un indicateur des effets bénéfiques de l'enseignement sur la société ou la consommation.*

*Ce chapitre s'achève par une description du contenu du rapport du Réseau B sur l'éducation et l'insertion professionnelle.*

\*

\*  \*

## 1.  The Rationale for Network B

Most people would agree that education plays an important role for both the individual and the whole society. Why education is important can, however, be viewed in different ways. Some people, probably the majority, emphasise the effects of education on job opportunities. In their view, the main purpose of education is to enhance the productivity and competitiveness of the individual in the labour market. For entire countries also, higher levels of education are expected to contribute to economic growth and job creation. Others are more inclined to stress the social and cultural benefits of education. These factors are also of great importance to both individuals and the society at large. They must therefore be kept in mind, even if the Network B indicators primarily focus on labour market and economic aspects of formal education.

There are several reasons for developing indicators on the links between education and the labour market. One reason is that countries generally spend a large amount of money on education. Questions that policy-makers often have to ask themselves are:

What are the results of all these investments in human capital? Do these investments really pay off for the individual and/or society? Does the economy grow faster, if more people receive a better education?

Other reasons for developing education indicators are connected to questions about how human and economic resources are being used, such as: Do men and women have the same opportunity to improve their skills through education? Do job opportunities improve for those who participate in adult education and training?

The indicators of INES Network B, together with the indicators developed by the other networks will, it is hoped, give useful indications about many relevant aspects, although, as yet, no variables reflecting the social and cultural benefits of education are included in the set of indicators.


## 2.   The Relevance to Policy

The main purpose of the Network B indicators is to provide tools for measuring the results of education and revealing problems in labour supply and demand. It has therefore been stressed throughout the project that the indicators should be relevant to policy-making. Policy-makers usually take a major interest in the level of completed education and training of the labour force and the general population. As industrial societies become increasingly knowledge-based and technology-driven, high-level skills, and the flexibility and adaptability of the labour force, become critical factors in economic development and job creation. In the context of rising unemployment in recent decades in many OECD Member countries, governments are increasingly directing their efforts towards enhancing the level of education and training of the labour force. They are seeking to ensure that individuals entering the labour market can do so with the abilities that are required to enable their countries to compete – not with low cost/low technology countries, but with countries characterised by high added-value manufacturing and services.

A movement towards employment in services and high-technology manufacturing in the post-war period has been accompanied by a changing pattern of skills formation in the labour force. The distribution of educational attainment varies between industries and occupational groups within countries. Indicators of completed education provide an indirect measure of the upper limit of the total supply to the labour market of persons with different levels of completed education. Against this background and the need for upgrading and updating of skills and competencies, policy-makers have shown interest in measuring the level of completed education and training of various groups in the labour force and the general population.


## 3.   A Conceptual Model

The OECD report *Making Education Count: Developing and Using International Indicators* (Tuijnman and Bottani, 1994), deals with conceptual and analytical issues in connection with education indicators. Topics such as how to choose indicators and how to interpret them are discussed, as well as the problems in data collection and the measurement of the indicators. One of the chapters of the report focuses especially on the task of Network B in studying labour market outcomes. The chapter, written by Russel W. Rumberger, is entitled "Labour market outcomes as indicators of educational performance". The author presents a conceptual model linking educational outputs to labour market outcomes. He shows the labour market outcomes to be results of an interaction between supply-side components (such as population characteristics and the education system) and demand-side components (the economic system). He describes three types of labour market outcome, namely: 1) employment outcomes; 2) workplace outcomes; and 3) social/political outcomes. Network B has so far concentrated mostly on the first group, employment outcomes.

The overall conclusion that Rumberger draws from his study is that "economic indicators can be useful in judging the performance of the education system, although the education system performs other functions besides the preparation of an adequately trained workforce". He also concludes that "a substantial body of empirical and theoretical research demonstrates a powerful linkage between educational outputs and a variety of economic and social outcomes", but that "the linkage is less straightforward and more complex than is commonly perceived".

## 4.   The Network's Background and Process of Work

Network B – led by Sweden – was set up in 1990, on the basis of the experience and the work carried out by an earlier network, active in the first phase of the INES project and dealing with outcomes of education (now Network A). There were three main motives for the establishment of Network B:

- the interaction between educational participation and employment participation is an important policy issue in relation to economic growth;
- education is assumed to provide an avenue for increased job opportunities for the individual;
- the labour market distribution of former students and the process of transition from school to work reflect the effectiveness and quality of education.

Network B comprises twenty countries. The lead country, Sweden, takes responsibility for communicating with and co-ordinating the efforts of the participating Member countries. The composition of the network has contributed to the progress of work. The National Delegates to the network represent a productive combination of administrators and statistical and policy experts in aspects of education and the labour market.

The network has met once or, during recent years, twice a year. Lately, the meetings have also been hosted by Member countries other than Sweden. Between these meetings, there has been intensive collaboration in data collection and the reporting of the indicators. A database with on-line facilities has been established at Statistics Sweden in the city of Örebro.

## 5. The Domain of Study

Network B's domain of study can be described as the intersection between the population, the education system and the labour market. The conditions and trends affecting this domain are regarded as of great general and political interest. Accordingly, there is heavy demand for statistical indicators useful for international comparisons and analyses. A highly relevant aspect in the domain of study of Network B is the transition from school to work and how different measures can promote this process. This is a major social and political issue in many OECD countries.

Another relevant aspect is the frequency of participation in continuing education and training among the labour force and the general adult population, and the amount of education and training received. Continuing education and training are important factors in skill formation, and interest in this area is growing as a result of an increased demand for competence in the labour market. The main task of Network B is to construct statistical indicators that can clearly and reliably describe the situation in various respects, and the relations among the different variables relevant to this domain of study. Examples of such relations are the long-term social, economic and labour market effects of education, and the impact of additional education on employment prospects.

The indicators defined by the network are intended to facilitate both national analyses and international comparisons. The differences observed internationally can provide an impetus for wider analyses and investigations of underlying causes, and for policy development at the national level.

## 6. The Indicators

Network B has developed statistical indicators for international comparisons of the educational attainment of the general population and the labour force, and other sub-sets of the population such as the employed and leavers from different levels of education. Sub-groups have been studied with respect to gender, age and level of education completed.

An indicator measuring the mean level of education in individual occupations and industries has been developed and calculated for a small number of selected occupations and industries.

In order to describe the economic outcomes of education, an indicator has been developed relating earnings from work to level of education. Here, much interesting and intriguing work remains to be done, as is shown in Chapter 7. One indicator has also been developed concerning leavers from different levels of the education system. This indicator was designed to show the entry of school-leavers into the labour market at a given time. The network has also developed an indicator intended for international comparisons of the frequency and amount of continuing education and training among the employed adult population.

## 7.   The Contents of this Volume

Short descriptions of the 17 indicators discussed by Network B, are given in Chapter 2, which also offers a technical commentary on the indicators and on data availability and data collection.

Chapter 3 gives an overview of the most important concepts and definitions used in the measurement of indicators developed by the network. They are mostly based on agreed international standards such as the International Standard Classification of Education (ISCED) and the International Standard Classification of Occupations (ISCO). In some cases, the network has also developed its own definitions, as far as possible based on combinations of existing international conventions and definitions.

Chapter 4 may be considered a "caveat" chapter, describing the contextual factors surrounding transition from education to the labour market. Such factors are, for example, the complex social, economic, geographical, historical and political circumstances defining the environment in which each country's education system and labour market operate. A good general knowledge of these factors is necessary for making adequate use of the information given by the indicators.

Chapter 5 deals with the changes in the conditions influencing the process of transition from school to work that have taken place since the mid-1970s. A major role in these changes is played by unemployment and the many different measures by which it is being combated by the countries. It is argued that the "traditional" data collection in this field should be supplemented by specially designed instruments or questionnaires related directly to the new circumstances that have emerged.

Education as a means of combating unemployment is a theme dealt with also in Chapter 6. The network has developed three indicators on education, employment and unemployment. The chapter discusses their relationships to several other education indicators. A proposal is then made that new indicators on the theme should look into the functioning of special programmes for the young unemployed.

One of the "core" indicators of Network B has, since the first issue of *Education at a Glance* (OECD, 1992), dealt with the links between the level of education and the level of earnings. For different reasons, though, there are still considerable limitations to this indicator. Chapter 7 offers a discussion of how this interesting indicator, which is of direct relevance to policy-making, can be elaborated.

The important issue of gender disparities is treated in both Chapter 8 and Chapter 9. Gender has been a breakdown variable in the data collection for many of the OECD indicators. In Chapter 8, the gender composition of the labour market by educational attainment is examined by the use of a range of indicators. This allows an assessment to be made of the influence of the education process on the labour market position of men and women. Chapter 9 gives an overview of the different techniques that have been applied by Network B to the calculation of an index of gender differences in educational attainment. None of the indices presented so far can meet all the desired criteria, but adjustments are proposed to overcome some of the problems identified.

One of the network's new indicators in the third edition of *Education at a Glance* (OECD, 1995) reflects the attempt to collect international data on continuing education and training for adults. Chapter 10 describes lifelong learning as an inevitable reality for the future development of education in the OECD Member countries. Thus, attention must be paid to the need for indicators which will permit international comparisons to be made in this field. The chapter shows the feasibility of measuring at least some aspects of continuing education and training using already available data sources, *e.g.* regular labour force surveys. It is argued that the challenge of developing quantitative measures of continuing education and training should now be taken seriously at both international and national levels.

In the last chapter, conclusions are presented from the network's activities. An analysis is offered of its strengths and weaknesses, and options for the future are put forward. It is suggested that priority should be given to continuing the work on a smaller scale and to trying to elaborate indicators on continuing education and training for adults and on the rate of return to investment in education, which are seen as particularly relevant to policy-making.

# References

OECD (1992), *Education at a Glance: OECD Indicators* (bilingual), 1st edition, CERI, Paris.

OECD (1995), *Education at a Glance: OECD Indicators*, 3rd edition, CERI, Paris.

TUIJNMAN, A.C. and BOTTANI, N. (Eds.) (1994), *Making Education Count: Developing and Using International Indicators*, OECD, CERI, Paris.

# Indicators of Network B
## *Indicateurs du Réseau B*

*by*

**Olof Jos** and **Kenny Petersson**
Statistics Sweden, Stockholm, Sweden

This chapter includes short descriptions of the 17 indicators developed by Network B in its domain of study: education and labour market destinations. Seven of the indicators were reported in the second edition of *Education at a Glance* (OECD, 1993). Three additional indicators have been included in the third edition (OECD, 1995), and the rest are still under development. The chapter also contains some technical comments about the indicators. The indicators reported concern educational attainment of the population, gender differences in education, labour force participation by education, educational attainment of workers, education and earnings, and participation in continuing education and training for adults. The chapter also includes comments on data availability and data collection strategy.

\*

\* \*

**Note de synthèse**

*Ce chapitre décrit brièvement les 17 indicateurs mis au point par le Réseau B dans son domaine d'étude intitulé « Éducation et insertion professionnelle ».*

*Les auteurs portent une grande attention aux sept indicateurs publiés dans les première et deuxième éditions de* Regards sur l'éducation. *Ces indicateurs sont les suivants : i) niveau général de formation ; ii) niveau de formation par sexe ; iii) indice de disparité des niveaux de formation par sexe ; iv) taux d'activité et niveau de formation ;*

v) *chômage des jeunes et des adultes;* vi) *chômage et niveau de formation;* vii) *niveau de formation et salaires.*

*Ce chapitre décrit aussi le développement de plusieurs indicateurs nouveaux. Trois autres indicateurs sont parus dans la troisième édition de* Regards sur l'éducation *(OCDE, 1995) :* i) *formation continue des adultes;* ii) *niveau de formation des travailleurs; et* iii) *situation au regard de l'activité des personnes sorties du système scolaire.*

*Enfin, ce chapitre mentionne plusieurs indicateurs encore à l'étude : le niveau de formation des inactifs, la répartition des actifs occupés par profession, le moment de l'entrée sur le marché du travail, les divers types de formation destinés aux jeunes chômeurs et les caractéristiques de la transition entre l'école et l'emploi. Dans la plupart des cas, il s'agit d'indicateurs provisoires, non pas du fait de difficultés techniques, mais parce que l'on manque généralement de données pour les calculer. C'est la raison pour laquelle ce chapitre traite aussi de questions telles que la disponibilité de données, les méthodes de collecte de données et la qualité des données recueillies par le Réseau B.*

\*

\*    \*

## 1.  Overview of Indicators

In its domain of study, education and labour market destinations, Network B has developed 17 indicators. Four of them belong to the cluster "Context of Education", ten to "Results of Education" and three to "Costs, Resources and School Processes".

These indicators for international comparisons refer to *the general population*, to *the labour force* and to other sub-sets of the population such as the employed and leavers from different levels of education. Sub-groups have been defined with respect to gender, age and level of education completed.

Concerning *the employed,* indicators measuring the mean level of education in individual occupations and industries have been developed and calculated for a small number of selected occupations and industries.

Concerning persons with *earnings from work*, indicators have been developed relating earnings from work to the level of education. In order to make international comparisons possible, these indicators have been defined as ratios between the earnings of groups with different educational attainments within each country. Sub-groups have been defined with respect to gender and age.

Indicators have also been developed concerning *leavers* from different levels of the education system. These indicators are designed to show the leavers' connection to the labour market at a given time after leaving the education system. Sub-groups have been defined with respect to gender and field of study.

The network has also defined and calculated indicators intended for international comparisons of the frequency and amount of *continuing education and training* among the adult population and among the employed.

The indicators are expressed in statistical terminology, variables of investigation or dependent variables. Each indicator is calculated for the whole target population in each country, usually persons from 25 to 64 years of age, and/or for specified parts of the population according to one or more breakdown variables, also called distribution variables.

The main distribution variables are gender, age and level of education attained, taken one at a time or in combination. The level of education is categorised according to the International Standard Classification of Education (ISCED) (*cf.* Chapter 3). In most cases, the following categories are distinguished:

- early childhood, primary and lower secondary education (ISCED 0/1/2),
- upper secondary education (ISCED 3),
- non-university tertiary education (ISCED 5), and
- university education (ISCED 6/7).

## 2.  Short Descriptions of the Indicators

A complete presentation of the indicators is found in the *Technical Manual for Education and Training Statistics* (OECD/EUROSTAT, forthcoming). The Manual contains a comprehensive and standardised presentation of each indicator.

Results from seven of the Network B indicators (*a-d* and *f-h* below) were reported in the second edition of *Education at a Glance* (OECD, 1993). Three additional indicators (*i, k* and *p*) have been included in the third edition of *Education at a Glance* (OECD, 1995). The rest of the indicators listed are still under development.

### *Indicators within the Cluster "Context of Education"*

a) *Percentage of the population that has attained a specific highest level of education* (C01 in *Education at a Glance*, 1995): this indicator can be seen as a measure of the outcome of the education system over a long period of time. The outcome is a result not only of formal schooling but also of adult education and training. However, demographic factors, such as migration, birth rates and mortality, also influence this outcome through their impact on the age structure.

b) *Gender differences in education: the percentage of women among those attaining specific levels of education* (C02A): this indicator shows to what extent women are under-represented or over-represented at certain levels of education.

c) *Gender differences in education: an index of gender dissimilarity* (C02B): this index provides a single measure of dissimilarity from a set of differences between men and women. High index values should invite further analysis and research.

d) *Labour force participation rate by level of educational attainment* (C11): according to conventions developed by the International Labour Organisation (ILO) and the OECD, the concept of "labour force" includes persons who are either employed, or unemployed but seeking a job and currently available for work.

**Indicators within the Cluster "Results of Education"**

e) *Employment rate*: the percentage of persons in different sub-sets of the population who are employed, according to ILO/OECD definitions.

f) *Unemployment rate by level of educational attainment* (R21): this indicator provides a general picture of the impact of additional education on employment prospects.

g) *Education and relative earnings from work* (R22A): in this indicator, the mean earnings from work for different levels of education are related to the mean earnings among persons with upper secondary education (ISCED 3). The calculations are based only on individuals with income from work during a specified reference period.

h) *Relative earnings from work of women compared with men* (R22B): this indicator relates the earnings from work among women to the earnings of work among men at the same level of education. In addition to inequities in earnings between men and women with the same educational qualifications, this indicator reflects such factors as occupation, amount of time worked and previous labour market experiences among men and women.

i) *Educational attainment of workers: an index of educational attainment of the employed by occupation* (R23): this indicator provides information on the number of years of education obtained by individuals working in certain occupations.

j) *Educational attainment by industry: an index of educational attainment of the employed by industry of employment* (R23B): this indicator provides information on the number of years of education that individuals who are employed within an industry/group of industries have received.

k) *Labour force participation rate for leavers from different levels of the education system* (R24A).

l) *Employment rate for leavers from different levels of the education system.*

m) *Unemployment rate for leavers from different levels of the education system* (R24B).

*Note:* The indicators *l)* and *m)* are parallel to the indicators *e)* and *k),* but here the target population consists of those who have left education within a certain period of time instead of the whole population.

n) *Relative unemployment rate for leavers* (R24C): this indicator relates the unemployment rate for leavers from different levels of the education system to the unemployment rate for the corresponding sections of the total labour force.

o) *Rate of participation in continuing education and training for adults*: continuing education and training includes all kinds of general and job-related education and training organised, financed or sponsored by public authorities, provided by employers or self-financed. The participation rate refers to a period of either four weeks or twelve months.

p) *Rate of participation in job-related continuing education and training for adults* (P08): job-related continuing education and training includes all organised, systematic education and training activities in which people take part in order to obtain knowledge and/or to learn new skills for their current or future job(s), to increase earnings, to improve job and/or career opportunities in their current or another field, and generally to improve their opportunities for advancement and promotion. The participation rate refers to a period of either four weeks or twelve months.

q) *Amount of job-related continuing education and training*: this indicator relates the total amount of time spent on job-related continuing education and training to the total hours of work for employed persons during a period of either four weeks or twelve months.

## 3. Some Indicators under Development

Network B has also discussed, developed and documented definitions for some additional indicators. One of these concerns the educational attainment of the part of population that is occupationally *inactive* but, subject to certain restrictions, is available for work. For the category of the *employed,* developmental work has been done on one indicator describing the occupational distribution of the employed by educational attainment, and on another indicator describing the sources of recruitment into employment.

Work has also been done on indicators describing the labour market situation for *young people.* In this field, indicators have been discussed and defined concerning 1) time of labour market entry; 2) training of different kinds for the young unemployed; and 3) characteristics of transition from school to work. These indicators are not yet ready for data collection, but they are described and documented in terms of definitions, rationale and relevance, data needed, calculation formulas and proposed breakdowns. At least some of them deserve further attention and developmental work.

## 4. Data Availability and Data Collection Strategy

Relevance to policy-making has been the first criterion in the choice and definition of indicators, but in order to enable data to be collected from existing sources it has in certain cases been necessary to make some adjustments to the initial definitions. The network has in these cases tried to find an optimal combination of relevance and data availability in as many Member countries as possible.

A general strategy has been to proceed to data collection at an early stage of the developmental work. This has been done in order to find out what data are available and to test the capacity of the countries to provide comparable data. The data collections have also included questions about data sources and data quality.

# References

OECD (1992), *Education at a Glance: OECD Indicators* (bilingual), 1st edition, CERI, Paris.

OECD (1993), *Education at a Glance: OECD Indicators* (bilingual), 2nd edition, CERI, Paris.

OECD (1995), *Education at a Glance: OECD Indicators*, 3rd edition, CERI, Paris.

OECD/EUROSTAT (forthcoming), *Technical Manual for Education and Training Statistics*, Paris.

*Chapter/Chapitre 3*

# Concepts and Definitions

## *Concepts et définitions*

*by*

**Thomas J. Healy**
Department of Education, Statistics Section, Dublin, Ireland
*and*
**Allan Nordin**
Statistics Sweden, Stockholm, Sweden

This chapter offers an overview of the most important concepts and definitions used in the indicators developed by Network B. Most of these concepts and definitions are based on accepted international standards such as the International Standard Classification of Education (ISCED), the International Standard Classification of Occupations (ISCO) and the International Standard Classification of Industry (ISIC). The standard definitions of labour force concepts are also of major importance for the Network B indicators.

Besides using these established concepts, Network B has developed its own definitions. In doing so the network has, as far as possible, used combinations of internationally developed concepts. Definitions of school leavers, of job-related continuing education and training, and of relative earnings from work are examples of definitions developed by the network. The gender aspect is dealt with by using special indices developed by the network and presented in detail in Chapter 8.

The network has been relying much on established definitions and concepts, but it has become clear that these are also sometimes difficult to apply in statistical indicators. The chapter gives examples of some of these difficulties, which have an impact on the indicator results.

\*

\*　　\*

# Note de synthèse

*Ce chapitre présente une vue d'ensemble des principaux concepts et définitions utilisés dans les indicateurs mis au point par le Réseau B. La plupart s'inspirent des normes adoptées à l'échelon international comme la Classification internationale type de l'enseignement (CITE), la Classification internationale type des professions (CITP) et la Classification internationale type, par industrie, de toutes les branches d'activité économique (CITI). Les définitions types des concepts relatifs à la population active proposées par l'OCDE et le Bureau international du travail sont également analysées.*

*Ces concepts reconnus sont très importants pour le Réseau B car l'idéal, pour procéder à des comparaisons valables entre pays, serait d'utiliser les statistiques de tous les pays qui correspondent aux mêmes définitions. Il faudrait pour cela que tous les pays interprètent de la même manière tous les concepts en question. Or, on s'est aperçu au cours des travaux que ce n'était pas toujours le cas. Les auteurs donnent plusieurs exemples de disparité dans l'interprétation que les pays donnent de concepts importants. Ils relèvent en particulier des divergences dans l'application de la CITE.*

*Outre ces concepts et définitions reconnus, le Réseau B a proposé ses propres définitions, tout en respectant, autant que possible, les conventions internationales et les notions convenues à l'échelon international. Les définitions de ce qu'il faut entendre par personne sortie du système scolaire, formation continue liée à l'emploi et salaires relatifs sont des exemples de définitions essentielles mises au point par le Réseau B.*

*Le Réseau B a dû se fonder dans l'ensemble sur des définitions et des concepts reconnus. Mais il est apparu que l'utilisation de concepts convenus pour la mise au point d'indicateurs présentait des inconvénients. Ce chapitre évoque un certain nombre de difficultés conceptuelles que présente le calcul d'indicateurs. Surmonter les difficultés qui influent sur les résultats est une priorité des travaux futurs sur les indicateurs dont s'occupe le Réseau B.*

\*

\*    \*

## 1. Introduction

This chapter contains a presentation of important concepts and definitions that are relevant for the indicators developed by Network B. Most of them are based on international standards. Others have been developed specially for the OECD project on International Indicators of Education Systems (INES).

The international standards used are among the best established in statistics on education and the labour market. Even so, the network has found that some of the definitions are difficult to adapt to the education systems in some countries. The ideal situation for meaningful comparisons between countries would be to use statistics for all countries based on the same definitions and standards. This in turn requires that the countries have the same understanding of all relevant concepts involved.

Even though countries have reached agreement on using certain standards, the application of the standards may differ between them. This may be because some standards can be more applicable to one type of society than to another. Other problems may be due to the fact that societies change over time. A standard classification may simply grow more or less obsolete.

## 2. International Standard Classification of Education (ISCED)

ISCED was adopted by the International Conference on Education in 1975. Later it was incorporated in the Revised Recommendation concerning the International Standardisation of Educational Statistics. ISCED has since the mid-1970s provided a basic conceptual framework for the collection, compilation and presentation of statistics on education at the international level. A description of ISCED is presented in the annex to this chapter.

### Changing Structures of Education

The education system has in many countries been changed considerably since the mid-1970s. New types of course have appeared, various types of training programme have been introduced, and various forms of apprenticeship or alternating training schemes are in operation. The greatly increased complexity and choice of programmes and modes of attendance in education pose a challenging task for the measurement of educational completion. The scope of education and training is not always clearly defined. Initial vocational training which takes place in educational institutions (at least for part of a student's total working time) can be more easily measured than continuing or further vocational education which takes place wholly in the enterprise where an individual is employed.

Both changes in the length of education at various levels, and the development of new curricula and programmes, make comparisons of completion between age-groups difficult in many cases. The classification of education in a labour force survey may reflect the current system of education, while the educational experience of the adult population surveyed dates back over a period of more than fifty years, during which the system will have seen some drastic changes. An additional problem is that a country may decide at one point in time to re-classify certain educational programmes or levels at a higher or lower ISCED level.

These and other changes have led to huge problems in classifying education programmes in accordance with the international standard. A growing need for revision of ISCED has been emphasised by the countries participating in Network B and has been requested several times by international organisations.

UNESCO, which has the main responsibility for the maintenance of ISCED, has started a process aiming at a revision of the system. In 1993, a survey was conducted in order to solicit views and suggestions from its Member States on a revision of ISCED. It is planned that a decision on this revision should be taken in the autumn of 1995, but it will certainly be some time before a new ISCED is in operation.

ISCED plays a crucial part in any project concerning comparative educational statistics. Also, the fact that many countries have problems in applying ISCED is a reason for a thorough look at the present system.

### Measuring Education

One problem with ISCED is that countries apply different criteria when classifying individuals at the various educational levels. Countries do not always classify diplomas and qualifications at the same ISCED level, even if they are obtained at roughly the same age or after a similar number of years of schooling. Some countries use the number of successfully completed years of schooling as the main criterion for classification. Others use information about diplomas obtained, and a third group uses both methods.

There are a number of alternative ways of *measuring* completed education and training. These may refer to competence, credentials or certification of achievement, or completed grade-years or levels. (The measurement of competence and student attainment levels in such areas as reading, mathematics and science is rightly dealt with by Network A of the INES project.)

At upper secondary level, some countries base their measurement of completion on grade-years completed, while others base their measurement on diploma/qualification obtained. Within the latter group, some define a pass rate; others count all candidates who present themselves for an examination or qualification as graduates or successful completers. ISCED is based implicitly on the notion of *hierarchy* in educational completion. However, not all countries share a one-dimensional hierarchy of qualifications or educational completion. At upper secondary level, with a wide range of programmes and courses, completed education may not be readily ordered in terms of a hierarchy.

Probably the most common measurement of completion among OECD countries is the credential or qualification achieved by individuals. However, qualifications such as diplomas, certificates and degrees may not readily be compared between countries even when they are awarded at a similar age and after a similar number of years of schooling. For example, it is possible that, in some countries, individuals who have completed four years of a four-year programme of general education at ISCED 3 but did not pass the final examination (because they either failed the examination or dropped out beforehand), are regarded as having not completed ISCED 3, whereas others who have successfully gained a diploma after only two years of a vocational programme, also at ISCED 3, are counted as successful graduates of that level. Moreover, an individual may obtain an ISCED 3 qualification at age 16 in one country, whereas in other countries the typical graduation age may be 18 or 19.

As an alternative measure, some use could be made of completed grade-years or levels. This entails measuring the number of grade-years completed (or the level of education attended prior to finishing initial education). Completion of a certain number of grade-years may or may not be accompanied by certification at the end of a programme.

The measurement of attendance at a particular ISCED level immediately prior to termination of education, in conjunction with completion of a hierarchically lower ISCED level, provides additional useful information on the level of education in the labour force. For example, an individual who proceeds to tertiary education upon completion of secondary education but drops out before completion of the tertiary level can be distinguished from persons who complete their education at upper secondary level and then leave education.

The total number of years of schooling of an individual may be measured starting from the beginning of ISCED 1 (or alternatively the compulsory school commencement age) as the basis for comparing ISCED level completion. For example, an individual who spent 12 grade-years in schooling in the United States (excluding kindergarten) has attained upper secondary education. After a further two years in college, he or she has attained ISCED 5 (sub-degree third level). After completion of four years after high school he or she is classified at ISCED 6 (university degree or equivalent).

Repetition of ''grade-years'' within a programme does not constitute additional time spent in education from the point of view of measuring the level attained. The ''grade-year'' approach is more easily adopted if a country has a well-defined grade-year structure of education and if the vast majority of students either drop out or pass from one stage of education to a higher level. However, measurement of grade-years completed may not be a very reliable guide to estimating level of completion with a given level of qualification. In vocationally oriented systems, the measurement of time spent in education is also not so readily attainable.

In a labour force survey, the basis for classification is the highest qualification reported by an individual. In some cases, a mixture of this approach and the number of grades or years completed is used. At the present time, it is impossible to synchronise the approaches completely because of the absence of data on a uniform basis across countries.

Many countries can readily distinguish between completed vocational training and general education in their labour force surveys. EUROSTAT defined vocational programmes as being tailored to preparation for a specific occupation or profession and as being either terminal or intended to facilitate further study only for the purpose of further preparation for the same occupation (EUROSTAT, 1992). In practice, some programmes are not easily classified in terms of the distinction between general and vocational education. Certain educational programmes do not lead to a defined occupation but provide an enhancement of a person's aptitude and preparedness for the labour market.

Individuals may also obtain two or more qualifications at what is considered to be the same ISCED level. For example, an individual may qualify with a diploma in general education at upper secondary level and then proceed to a vocational programme equally considered to be at upper secondary level. Multiplicity of programmes at a given ISCED level may present measurement problems in terms of the completed education and training of the labour force, especially where vocational qualifications obtained in previous decades may not be easily allocated to a particular ISCED level. Over time, the nature and content of vocational programmes may change so that recording information on completed vocational programmes for the adult population may present particular problems. For example, apprenticeship training may have become increasingly formalised, so that older workers in the labour force who completed apprenticeship training may not have received a formal qualification or have attended school or college on release from employment.

### Proposed Changes in the ISCED Classification

During all meetings of Network B there have been discussions about problems with the ISCED classification. There appears to be a convergence of views of what the principal problems are for ISCED definitions. However, there is a variety of solutions and proposed changes. In the spring of 1994, proposals for changes were presented to the network, reflecting the response of a number of countries to a UNESCO questionnaire issued in 1993 concerning the need for revision of ISCED.

ISCED was originally designed for classification of programmes and courses of education, not for classification of individuals. Some countries find this to be the root of the problem. Classifying persons is more complicated than classifying courses.

The changes proposed in spring 1994 start with the *definition of education*. The present definition says that education comprises "organised and sustained communication designed to bring about learning". According to one proposal, the definition should be expanded to include mention of preparation for the labour market or upgrading of skills and knowledge relevant to employment in the labour market.

The present ISCED definition makes a distinction between "regular school and university education" on one hand and "adult education" on the other. According to the proposals, this distinction is not clear enough and the criterion of regular education "lacks analytical power". It causes problems for the notion of apprenticeship. It is proposed that the distinction between "regular education" and "adult education" should be dropped.

When it comes to the ISCED categories, some countries argue for an expansion of the number of levels. There is, however, a lack of agreement about the criteria for this classification. There is one proposal that the new sub-levels should be based on the nominal duration of a programme. In another proposal, the duration of education is proposed as the criterion for determining ISCED levels 0 to 3 only. For tertiary education, equivalence of degrees is suggested.

There are also different ideas between countries about how to classify tertiary education. In one proposal, ISCED level 7 is assigned to "education at the third level, of the type that leads to the last university degree before the doctorate or equivalent". A new level 8 is then proposed for doctorates.

### Data Sources

The main sources of information on completed level of education are population censuses or labour force surveys (including the Current Population Surveys in the United States). In the European Union, a labour force survey is undertaken annually in the spring. Each Member State uses a survey questionnaire which is similar, although not identical, to that used in other European Union countries.

As in all household surveys, the results are subject to both sampling and non-sampling errors. The latter are more difficult to measure and may be more substantial than realised.

Non-sampling errors arise due to factors such as the inability or unwillingness of respondents to provide correct answers or even any answer at all (non-response), mistakes by interviewers when filling in survey documents, mis-coding, etc. The response of persons to a survey may be influenced by the political or social circumstances at the time of the interview. Sampling errors arise from the fact that a sample and not a full census is taken of households. At a national level and for broad aggregates, sampling errors are likely to be small, so that the survey estimates are likely to be quite accurate.

However, detailed cross-classifications by age, ISCED level or labour force status, especially at sub-national level (regions and provinces), entail larger sampling errors. Comparability of results between countries may be affected by such factors as adjustments in population figures due to new population censuses and differences in the reference period used to measure labour force status.

In the European Union, the labour force surveys of Member States contain information on education and training received during the four weeks prior to the survey interview. This information is classified according to whether the person received training in a school or college only, in a working environment only, or in a dual training situation. Additional information is recorded about the purpose of the training or education received in the previous four weeks. Data are also collected on the total length of training and on the highest completed level of education according to ISCED. In some countries, these data are collected separately for the highest level of completed general education and vocational training.

## 3. International Standard Classification of Occupations (ISCO-88)

### *The Design and Structure of ISCO-88*

The International Standard Classification of Occupations (ISCO-88), developed by the International Labour Office, was adopted in November 1987, replacing ISCO-68. ISCO-88 has three aims, namely:

- to facilitate international communication about occupations by supplying statisticians with tools to make national occupational data available internationally;
- to make it possible for international occupational data to be produced in a form which can be useful for research as well as for specific decision-making and action-oriented activities, such as those connected with international migration or job placement; and

Table/Tableau 3.1.

**The structure of the International Standard Classification of Occupations 1988 (ISCO-88)**

Major groups with skill levels and number of sub-groups

*Structure de la classification internationale type des professions, 1988 (CITP)*

| Major groups | Sub-major groups | Minor groups | Unit groups | ISCO skill level |
|---|---|---|---|---|
| 1. Legislators, senior officials and managers | 3 | 8 | 33 | – |
| 2. Professionals | 4 | 18 | 55 | 4th |
| 3. Technicians and associate professionals | 4 | 21 | 73 | 3rd |
| 4. Clerks | 2 | 7 | 23 | 2nd |
| 5. Service workers and shop and market sales workers | 2 | 9 | 23 | 2nd |
| 6. Skilled agricultural and fishery workers | 2 | 6 | 17 | 2nd |
| 7. Craft and related trades workers | 4 | 16 | 70 | 2nd |
| 8. Plant and machine operators and assemblers | 3 | 20 | 70 | 2nd |
| 9. Elementary occupations | 3 | 10 | 25 | 1st |
| 0. Armed forces | 1 | 1 | 1 | – |
| Total | 28 | 116 | 390 | |

- to serve as a model for countries developing or revising their national occupational classifications. ISCO-88 is, however, not intended to replace any existing national classification of occupations.

ISCO-88 is based on two main concepts: the kind of work performed (job) and the skill level. The job is defined as a set of tasks and duties executed by one person, whereas the skill is defined as the ability to carry out the tasks and duties of a given job. In ISCO-88, four broad skill levels are defined in terms of the educational categories and levels of ISCED. However, this does not imply that the skills necessary to perform the tasks and duties of a given job can be acquired only through formal education. Informal training and experience can also give the same skills.

The hierarchical structure of ISCO-88 consists of ten major groups at the top level of aggregation, subdivided into 28 sub-major groups, 116 minor groups, and 390 unit groups (see Table 3.1).

## Data Collection

At the beginning of the second phase of the INES project, Network B developed an indicator called ''Occupational Distribution of the Employed by Educational Attainment'' (indicator R23 in the third edition of *Education at a Glance*, 1995). The intention was to illustrate the occupational distribution in terms of ISCO-88 categories. The number of network Member countries was then 18. When the first ''full-scale'' data collection was carried out in the spring of 1991 (a pilot having been arranged some months earlier), 13 out of the 18 Member countries could provide data on occupations, but only five of them by using ISCO-88. Most of the others made use of the ISCO 68 nomenclature, but not in a totally homogeneous way.

During the 1991 data collection, data for 1989 (and also for 1984 for some indicators) were gathered. It was of course not surprising that so few countries had started applying ISCO-88 at that time. But even during the 1993-94 data collection the number of reporting countries was not much higher than in 1991. By April 1994, only eight countries had reported occupational data based on ISCO-88. The reasons for not reporting could be of different kinds. In some cases, the data were just not available for some reason. In other cases, the national classifications of occupations were not easily transferred into the two-digit and three-digit ISCO-88 groups that were asked for in the questionnaire.

Even when data have been delivered, the preliminary results indicate that there can be substantial differences in content in the groups between countries. When data are stored in aggregated form, it will sometimes be difficult (or even impossible) to report data for specific groups.

The twelve European Union countries use a modified version of ISCO-88 called ISCO-88(COM). The two versions do not differ very much.


## 4.  The Standard ILO/OECD Definitions of Labour Force Concepts

The standard definitions of the ILO/OECD (ILO, 1990) form the framework of countries' labour force surveys and to some extent also of censuses, although some countries apply definitions that differ slightly from the standard because, for example, of local variations in economic or cultural structure.

According to these definitions, the *labour force* (or the "economically active population") comprises persons in employment or unemployment.

The *employed* comprise all persons who during a specified brief period, either one week or one day, were in paid employment or self-employment. Unpaid domestic activities and voluntary community services are not counted as economic activity by the employed. *Unemployed persons* are all individuals who, during a brief specified reference period, were without work, were currently available for work and were *actively* seeking work (*i.e.* had taken specific steps in a given reference period to seek employment). Finally, as is shown in Figure 3.1, all persons who are not classified as employed or unemployed are defined as "economically inactive" or not in the labour force.

Most countries conduct household-based labour force surveys in which detailed information on persons aged 15 (or 16) and over is recorded, including data on completed education. In most cases, this survey provides the main source of information on the completed education of the population over 14 (or 15) years of age.

The inclusion of all persons in the category of labour force who undertook at least one hour of paid employment means that many persons undertaking part-time or casual

37

Figure/*Graphique* 3.1. **Basic classification into employed and unemployed according to international definitions**

*Classification de base des actifs occupés et des chômeurs selon les définitions internationales*

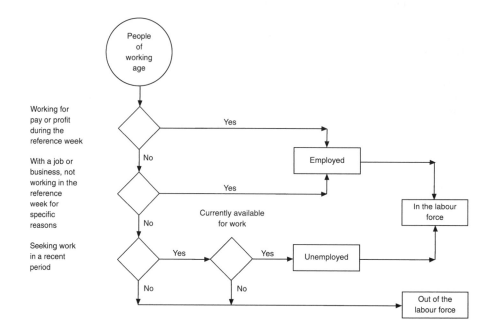

*Source:* ILO and OECD.

employment are included. Moreover, persons in part-time employment (even if for one hour a week during the specified reference period) are classified as being in employment, although they may actively be seeking full-time work. For this reason, the full extent of unemployment may be understated to the extent that some persons in part-time employment are under-employed.

There are variations between OECD countries in the definition of persons in part-time employment. Among the countries of the European Union, persons are classified in the labour force surveys as being in part-time employment on the basis of their own assessment, irrespective of the actual number of hours of work.

## 5. International Standard Classification of Industry (ISIC)

ISIC was adopted in 1968 by the United Nations. In the network's 1994 data collection it became clear that although countries sometimes have similar denominations for groups of industries, the content of the groups may differ considerably. One example is the list of industries that was sent out in connection with the data collection concerning "Educational Attainment of Workers by Industry of Employment": the industries listed and the codes for the different groups were said to refer to ISIC, but did not coincide with the list published by the United Nations.

The Member States of the European Union use a coding standard called NACE (General Industrial Classification of Economic Activities within the European Communities) when they report data to EUROSTAT on employment by industry. There are obvious similarities between NACE and ISIC, but also clear differences. Perhaps the most important difference between the two standards is that NACE has an energy sector (energy and water = NACE 1) which contains more activities than the energy sector of ISIC (electricity, gas and water = ISIC 4). At a two-digit level, though, the two standards are comparable.

## 6. Definitions Developed by Network B

In some cases, Network B has developed its own definitions by using, as far as possible, combinations of internationally accepted concepts. These definitions are presented in this section, together with some of the related problems and the solutions adopted by the network.

### *School Leavers*

During the second phase, Network B developed two different sets of indicators on school leavers, one dealing with the labour force status of school leavers in the long term and the short term (R24 in *Education at a Glance*, 1995), the other dealing with transition characteristics for leavers. (The official title of the latter was "Labour Market Entry". It was designed to measure how long it takes for different groups to get a stable job.) This set of indicators has not yet been developed to a stage where it may be considered ready for data collection.

Network B has also developed specific definitions of school leavers. To be classified as school leavers, individuals have to satisfy two conditions, namely: not being enrolled in full-time education or training at the beginning of a certain school year (the reference year); and having successfully completed a certain level of education in the course of the school year preceding the reference year.

### *Continuing Education and Training (CET)*

Network B has defined "continuing education and training" (CET) as all kinds of general and job-related education and training organised, financed or sponsored by authorities, provided by employers or self-financed. Included in the definition are training courses on the job as well as off the job, and courses for adults leading to an educational qualification. Military training and full-time studies at ISCED levels 5, 6 and 7 are excluded.

Network B's work focuses on links between the education system and the labour market. Job-related continuing education and training are therefore of special interest to the network as well as to policy-makers. Continuing vocational training provides the individual with new qualifications that are intended to lead to a more stable position in the labour market or to a higher position in the job hierarchy.

It is of course difficult to distinguish between job-related and non job-related courses. A foreign language class, for example, can be a leisure course for one person and a job-related course for another. The only people who can make this classification are the individuals who attend the courses: it is more difficult to determine from register data, which are not based on enquiries among the individuals, whether the courses attended are job-related or not.

Up until the 1993/94 data collection, information about job-related CET focused on those in employment. In the further development of this indicator, thought should be given to whether persons who are unemployed or outside the labour force could be included as well. Persons belonging to these groups could attend the same types of course in order to improve their qualifications and thus gain a position in the labour market.

### Relative Earnings from Work

Education represents an investment in knowledge and skills. The returns to this investment can be analysed under two headings, the social returns and returns to the individual. The social returns have to do with the extra resources that can be created in the society by virtue of having a more skilled population. These returns can be economic as well as "cultural". The approach that Network B has taken so far is, however, to concentrate on the returns to individuals.

The earnings advantage that more highly educated persons have compared to others can be viewed as part of the economic return to this investment. Network B has developed an indicator measuring the earnings for the different ISCED levels related to the earnings of those with upper secondary education (ISCED 3) as their highest education.

In the first edition of *Education at a Glance* (OECD, 1992), the mean earnings were calculated as follows. All the earnings of people in the age-group 45-64 at a given level of education were divided by the total number of people at the same level. That means that all persons, employed as well as unemployed and people not in the labour force, were included in the calculation. The purpose was to sum up all types of labour market outcomes into one single measure. Many factors influenced this measure, such as the opportunity to get a job, the opportunity or propensity to work full-time or part-time and the differences in hourly earnings between the groups.

In the second and third editions (OECD, 1993, 1995), the definition of mean earnings was somewhat altered compared to that used in 1992. In the newer calculations of mean earnings, those with an income from work were included and those without an income from work were excluded. The income differences between various ISCED groups due to differences in employment opportunities were thus narrowed in *Education at a Glance* (OECD, 1993 and 1995). A further discussion of this indicator and an analysis of findings reported in *Education at a Glance* (OECD, 1993) is found in Chapter 7.

## 7. Special Indices Used by Network B

Three indices have been used as indicators by Network B. Two of them deal with gender differences, namely the *index of gender dissimilarity* and the *index of gender difference.* These indices are defined, discussed and analysed in Chapter 8. The third index deals with the amount of education among employees in selected occupations and industries. This index will be described here.

### Index of Educational Attainment

Network B has developed two indicators on the average number of years of school-ing that different groups of employed persons have attained. One of the indicators deals with occupations (R23A), the other with industries (R23B). Both indicators use one characteristic of educational attainment – years of schooling – to compute an index of educational attainment. The purpose of the indicators is to summarise a great deal of information on the educational attainment of the employed in a variety of occupations and industries in OECD countries.

The use of "time spent" in the system based on the "typical" ISCED duration for each country has the advantage of providing a single numerical measure of educational completion for the labour force as a whole, or for sub-groups by age, occupation and industry. However, the imputation of an average full-time duration for each ISCED level in each country presents some problems.

A survey of countries which were participating in Network B in early 1994 reveals that the cumulative duration of schooling up to the end of ISCED 2 does not vary greatly between countries, while the duration of ISCED 3 and higher levels varies considerably. Moreover, there are significant variations in average duration within ISCED levels in many countries. This applies particularly at tertiary levels 6 and 7, where different modes of attendance and fields of study make it difficult to arrive at an average cumulative duration of study for a given country which can be empirically based and which is appropriate in the analysis of particular sub-groups or occupations. For example, country A may have an average duration of 3.5 years for ISCED level 6 and country B may have an average duration of 5 years. However, for engineering programmes at ISCED 6, the average duration of courses may be 5 years in both countries. It would therefore be inappropriate to compare the educational attainment of engineers in both countries by reference to an average duration of 3.5 years and 5 years respectively.

The measurement of completion of tertiary education may also be distorted by varying interpretations of ISCED 6 and 7 by countries in classifying university degree programmes. Some countries make no distinction between these two ISCED levels. Others take a very literal interpretation of ISCED by classifying all post-graduate

Master's degree programmes and equivalents at ISCED 7, even though in some cases these programmes are completed in one to two years after a relatively short initial university degree programme of only three or four years.

The biggest difficulty in using a measure of "time spent" in education from the compulsory school commencement age is probably the existence of multiple programmes at some ISCED levels, especially at ISCED 3 but also at ISCED 5 and 6. Many students completing general education at upper secondary level proceed to a vocational programme at the same level.

Significant variations in average duration by ISCED level may also exist between different age-groups. For example, a country may have extended the length of upper secondary courses from three to four years on average in the 1960s. This would affect the comparisons of different age-groups within a country and would lead to a bias in international comparisons of occupations or industries if the age structure of the labour force in the countries differed significantly.

The measurement of average duration of study by ISCED level is also made difficult by the variations in the length of what countries regard as part-time courses *vis-à-vis* what they regard as full-time courses.

Measurement of time with reference to years of schooling may be distorted by such factors as variations in the quality of education between levels and between countries, as well as differences in the total time spent in tuition (depending on the length of the school year and the school day). Hence, over a period of 12 years of schooling, it is possible for two countries to have significantly different cumulative totals of hours spent in classroom instruction.

The introduction of additional semesters in the academic year at tertiary level means that individuals may complete a four-year programme in two or three years by following a more intensive programme of studies.

## 8. Conclusion

Internationally accepted concepts are very important for the work of Network B, since the ideal situation would be to use statistics for all countries that were based on the same definitions. However, in the course of the work it became clear that there is no universal understanding of all the relevant concepts involved, even when there are standard international classifications such as ISCED, ISCO and ISIC. Consultations are indeed under way to revise the ISCED categories themselves.

Besides using established definitions, Network B put forward its own proposals for definitions of school leavers, continuing education and training, and relative earnings from work. The network also used three indices as indicators, derived from available data. Where possible, these definitions and indices adhered to international conventions and internationally agreed concepts. Nevertheless, it is evident that the application of established concepts to statistical indicators has certain limitations. Overcoming the conceptual difficulties which influence the validity and comparability of the results is a priority for further work in the domain of study of Network B.

# Description of ISCED

In a UNESCO publication on the International Standard Classification of Education (ISCED), the following description is given:

"ISCED is based on two principal educational criteria, viz. the *level* and the subject-matter *content* of study. In the ISCED system the most detailed unit of education is a course. A selection of one or more courses, called a programme, constitutes the smallest unit for classification, programmes that are related in terms of level and major subject-matter content being grouped into programme groups. Programme groups are further aggregated into fields made up of programme groups related to the same general subject matter or area. The fields and programme groups are designated within levels, which consist of categories representing broad steps of educational progression from very elementary to more complicated learning experience. ISCED is therefore, a three-stage classification system providing successive subdivisions from level to field to programme group (UNESCO, 1976)."

The same UNESCO publication gives the following description of the classification of levels:

"Seven categories of education, based upon level, a residual category for education not definable by level, and when needed, a position for individuals having no education, are incorporated into the ISCED structure as follows:

0   Education preceding the first level

1   Education at the first level

2   Education at the second level, first stage

3   Education at the second level, second stage

5   Education at the third level, first stage, of the type that leads to an award not equivalent to a first university degree

6   Education at the third level, first stage, of the type that leads to a first university degree or equivalent

7   Education at the third level, second stage, of the type that leads to a postgraduate university degree or equivalent

9   Education not definable by level (UNESCO, 1976)."

# References

EUROSTAT (1992), *Labour Force Survey – Methods and Definitions,* Office for Official Publications of the European Communities, Luxemburg.

ILO (1990), *Surveys of Economically Active Population, Employment, Unemployment and Underemployment – An ILO Manual on Concepts and Methods*, Geneva.

OECD (1992), *Education at a Glance: OECD Indicators* (bilingual), 1st edition, CERI, Paris.

OECD (1993), *Education at a Glance: OECD Indicators* (bilingual), 2nd edition, CERI, Paris.

OECD (1995), *Education at a Glance: OECD Indicators*, 3rd edition, CERI, Paris.

UNESCO (1976), *International Standard Classification of Education,* Paris.

# Contextual Factors Surrounding Transitions from Education to the Labour Market

## *Facteurs contextuels influant sur le passage de la formation à la vie active*

*by*

### Kenneth D. Bennett

Education and Culture Division, Statistics Canada, Ottawa, Canada

The indicators which have been developed by Network B are intended to inform the user of the interactions between education and the labour markets within Member countries. The purpose of this chapter is to point out to the reader some of the more apparent contextual factors which he or she should bear in mind when using the measures produced by the network.

The indicators being developed by Network B are intended to inform the user of the interactions between education and the labour markets within Member countries and to enable comparisons to be made between countries or regions. For example, some indicators attempt to provide the reader with summary measures which reveal the gains derived from education in terms of its impact on the labour market status of the population. Others focus on the ease or difficulty with which individuals are able to make the transition from the period in their life when they are primarily concerned with obtaining an education to one in which they are seeking to establish themselves in employment. The relative quality of the employment which is available with different levels of education may be quantified by the income obtained or the ability to find and hold permanent or long-term employment. Or, the skill levels available to perform certain jobs or which are found within certain industries may be gauged by the average educational attainment levels of the persons presently employed in those areas, and this may help to determine areas where there are skills shortages which could affect a nation's competitiveness.

However well defined these indicators are, they reveal only a superficial amount of information about the complex social, economic, geographical, historical and political circumstances that define the environment in which each country's education system and labour market operate. And even if one were to have access to the full range of indicators which are being produced by the INES project, they would still probably give insufficient information for the user to be able to place the differences in results between countries in their proper context. It is only with a good general knowledge of these factors that the user can make worthwhile use of the information contained in the indicators.

The objective of this chapter is not to identify all of these various differences which exist between countries in each of the topic areas mentioned above, or to quantify their impact on the indicators' values. That chore would be too difficult even if one were only to attempt to enumerate them. Instead, it will try to note some of the more global characteristics which differentiate countries and to show how these factors may affect the relationship between education and the labour market within a country. The material presented is not intended to be exhaustive but merely indicative of the issues which need to be considered when the indicators are used. Some of the later chapters which deal with specific indicators touch a little more closely upon those factors which significantly affect the outcomes observed for those indicators.

\*

\*     \*

### Note de synthèse

*Le propos de ce chapitre est d'attirer l'attention du lecteur sur certains des facteurs contextuels les plus évidents dont il faut tenir compte lorsqu'on utilise les indicateurs mis au point par le Réseau B. L'analyse n'est pas exhaustive, mais elle entend donner une idée des caractéristiques plus générales qui différencient les pays. Ce chapitre montre aussi que ces caractéristiques peuvent influer sur le lien entre la formation et le marché du travail.*

*Les indicateurs construits par le Réseau B sont destinés à informer l'utilisateur de l'interaction entre la formation et le marché du travail dans les pays Membres de l'OCDE. Même si ces indicateurs sont précis, ils ne fournissent que des informations superficielles sur le contexte social, géographique, historique et politique, complexe qui caractérise l'environnement dans lequel s'inscrivent les systèmes d'enseignement et de formation et les marchés du travail de chaque pays. En outre, même si l'on avait accès à toute la série d'indicateurs établis dans le cadre du projet de l'OCDE sur les indicateurs internationaux des systèmes d'enseignement (INES), ceux-ci ne seraient pas encore suffisamment précis pour que l'utilisateur puisse replacer dans leur contexte les dispa-*

*rités des résultats d'un pays à l'autre. Seule une solide connaissance générale de bon nombre de ces facteurs sous-jacents peut permettre à l'utilisateur de tirer judicieusement parti des informations que renferment les indicateurs.*

*

\*    \*

## 1. The General Indicators Model

"Education systems and the results they produce do not exist in a vacuum; they are the product of a complex historical process and are influenced by many factors in the surrounding environment. While some of these factors are malleable and can be optimised, many others are given and cannot be changed through educational policy. An analysis of education must therefore be informed by an appreciation of the educational processes employed and the financial and other resources expended, against a background of contextual factors in the environment of education systems, schools and students." (*Education at a Glance,* OECD, 1993, p. 22).

Most models of general education indicators distinguish between inputs, process and outcomes, all conditioned by environmental or surrounding contextual aspects. *Inputs* represent what education systems start with (the students, the teachers, the schools, the types of instruction and the facilities); *process* refers to what education does with the inputs (programmes and processes such as curricula, instructional organisation, use of technology and student/teacher time, school climate, etc.; and *outcomes* are the cognitive (achievement) and non-cognitive effects of education on students (work, incomes, skills, attitudes and behaviours). The environmental variables represent the context within which the education occurs, as shown in Figure 4.1.

The surrounding context includes demographic, geographical, economic, socio-cultural and social factors, and society's values and goals for education. Historical and political issues are also important: "Any understanding of the effects or outcomes of education must be informed by the educational processes employed and the resources (fiscal and human) deployed, against the background of contextual factors in the environment of school or of education systems" (Nuttall, 1992).

Inputs and processes can be altered, but the context cannot generally be manipulated by policies within the scope of education systems.

The following sections take up each of the above contextual areas in turn, briefly describe its significance, provide examples of its range of characteristics, and suggest what its impact may be on the results of the indicators; it is important to be aware of differences caused by contextual factors when interpreting a specific indicator. The

Figure/*Graphique* 4.1. **The general indicators model**
***Le modèle d'indicateurs généraux***

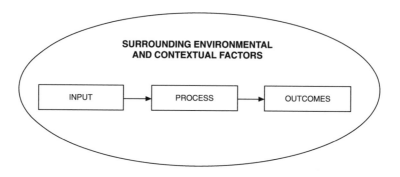

*Source:* Statistics Canada.

contextual areas delineated are not mutually exclusive. A number of them are inter-related, and changes in any one would probably result in adjustments in a number of others.

## 2. Demography

Demographic characteristics represent a significant defining aspect of nations and have played a major role in the expansion of education systems. All other things being equal, variations in absolute population numbers and their distributions by age, for example, will affect transitions between education and the labour market. Some of the aspects which can be expected to make a difference are changes in population size (birth rates, immigration); population density and distribution; age distribution; and ethnic and religious composition.

In countries with similar rates of employment growth, the ease of transition between education and work may vary according to rates of *population increase*. Nations with low rates of population increase will be more able to absorb graduates into the labour market, other things being equal, than nations with high rates of population increase. Those which use immigration as a means of ensuring certain levels of population growth or to meet short-term labour requirements could also expect this to have an influence, particularly if the intake levels are large relative to the overall size of the population, or if the incoming population has certain characteristics in its age composition, dependent ratio, skill levels, and language.

Countries which have a *small population* distributed over a relatively *large geographical area* may not be able to afford the capital cost of the facilities required to provide all their population with the full range of educational services. Furthermore, when limited facilities are provided, participation may not reach high levels because of the cost or other difficulties of travelling to the location of those facilities. This situation may be changing with the availability of newer technologies, but is probably an artifact in the indicators which are currently being calculated.

The *age distribution* of the population is particularly important. Countries with large numbers of young people and relatively few in middle age would probably experience transitional problems very different from those of countries with small populations of young people and large groups of middle-aged. There does appear to be an association between the size of the youth population (15-24) and youth unemployment; countries with larger populations of young people tend to have higher youth unemployment rates and vice versa, with a few exceptions (*Education at a Glance*, OECD, 1993, indicators C3 and C6).

A country whose population contains a large native minority *sub-population* from an ethnic or religious society may attempt to address the cultural and moral needs of this population by providing for an alternative education system. The presence of such parallel systems could have an impact on the aggregate results for a number of the indicators produced by the INES project in the inputs and process areas as well as in the outcomes area. Certain indicators on education and the labour market might be affected if these parallel systems result in different termination points, or in the development of unique skills or employment expectations, or if they have different funding or access arrangements. Such differences could cause dissimilarities between the skills of the leavers from the majority and minority programmes.

## 3. Geographical Factors

Basic variations in geography can make a difference in the relationship between education and the labour market. Some of the factors to be considered within this category are regional variations, resources, and proximity to trading partners.

Countries composed of a number of *regional* economies with very different industrial, occupational and employment structures, and considerable differences in educational structures, could also be expected to show results different from those of countries with more uniform economies. These differences would be further exaggerated if there were varying patterns of mobility (or retention) between regions due to some of the demographic factors noted above, or distance or physical barriers. Comparisons with other nations at the same level of development and population size, but with a concentrated national economy and few barriers to mobility, would have to be made with caution.

Similarly, it would not be appropriate to make direct comparisons between countries undergoing substantial rural-to-urban migration with those already highly urban in nature. The differences between rural and urban education and rural and urban labour markets would influence the relationships between education and employment.

There are also geographical aspects of industrial organisation that may affect the links between education and work. One country may achieve a competitive advantage in the world economy by capitalising on its natural *resources,* while another may import resources and export finished products. Such factors may influence education and its links with occupations and employment. Comparisons between countries, therefore, need to be informed by the natural resource base of those countries.

Lastly, *proximity to major trading partners*, or the development of relatively integrated trading blocks, could have significant impact on the demands placed on the education systems of Member countries and their outputs. Those which have achieved high levels of integration, including the flow of labour and services, would probably tend to evolve similar education systems, while those which have not, might retain different systems, leading to a distinctiveness in the results of some of the indicators.

## 4.   Economic Factors

A major characteristic which differentiates nations is their level of economic development. The gross domestic product (GDP) per capita of OECD countries varies between $2 813 and $17 920 (1991 US$) (OECD, 1993, indicator C7). However, because countries with a low GDP also tend to have the highest percentage of youth in the population there are even larger differences in GDP per young person than in GDP per capita. Wealthy nations are able to dedicate more money to education and training than less wealthy nations (OECD, 1993, p. 53).

In addition to absolute differences in the level of economic development, variation in rates of economic growth can be expected to influence transitions. Annual growth rates in some countries were over 3 per cent for the period 1981-91, while others had an annual growth in GDP per capita of below 1.5 per cent (OECD, 1993, p. 53).

Besides these somewhat generalised differences between economies, several other features may play an important role and impinge on the results of the indicators. Among these features are the choice between planned and market economies (or government involvement in markets); the balance between goods-producing and service-producing industries; the presence and influence of multi-national firms; membership of trading blocks; and debt/deficits and the availability of funding.

## 5.   Socio-cultural Factors

Educational outcomes such as cognitive, labour market and non-economic attitudes and behaviours are all influenced by broad social and cultural environments.

In some countries, the participation of greater numbers of women in the labour market might provide role models and other incentives for young women to enter non-traditional fields of study. This might have the dual benefit of reducing the supply of labour in the traditional occupations and raising the overall quality of that supplied in non-traditional professions, resulting in better transitions overall. The availability of child care, in the form of day care or early childhood education programmes, would seem to be a contributor to female participation rates, and is therefore another factor which needs to be recognised in this context.

Some jurisdictions may use factors such as minimum wage rates, differentiated for young people and adults, to control or encourage entry into the labour market. Subsidies in the form of tax reductions, for instance, may be offered to employers to take on larger numbers of inexperienced workers. The length of study required to enter certain fields might also be used as a means of governing the numbers seeking to enter those fields and of controlling the flow of entry into work.

A number of jurisdictions may use national service as a means of facilitating the transition into the labour market, or at least of offering a means of transition for certain segments of the population. This sort of service could be seen as an extension of "training" in some sense, since participants develop skills which are not unlike those which might be attained in "co-op" or internships in other jurisdictions. An important consideration is the different impact such service might have on the indicator results for men and women.

A number of other factors may impinge on labour market entry. In some countries there may be strong peer, ethnic and community networks or family practices which facilitate transition to labour markets. In other countries, these support networks and linkages may be less well developed, or have been abandoned, with labour market entry being more a question of competition on an open market, or of chance.

Some countries may be diverse in terms of the linguistic, ethnic and cultural composition of the population, possibly because of immigration. Others may be relatively homogeneous. The education systems of heterogeneous nations have a task very different from those whose population base is homogeneous. Absorption into the labour force will also be affected, particularly if there are rapid changes in cultural composition. The strength of class or social structures within the population will also have some impact upon the labour market transition characteristics of members of groups in the society.

## 6. Additional Social Factors

Apart from the socio-cultural factors already mentioned, other social aspects can also make a great deal of difference in education, and consequently, may affect transitions to the labour market. These are, for example, access, public support (the involvement of parents, volunteers and business; and public expectations and satisfaction); choice; and mobility.

There are different beliefs about the desirable *accessibility* of education, particularly post-secondary education, which may restrict the supply of graduates to the labour market. According to one set of beliefs, access to advanced education should be restricted to the best academic performers. Post-secondary access, therefore, may be highly selective, admitting few students and dedicating substantial resources to their success. These "elite" systems can be contrasted with mass or open-access systems, in which advanced education is seen as a universal right or opportunity that should be extended to all. The open-access systems admit many more students but their resources are spread more thinly.

Data on participation rates show considerable variation between countries, and the impact on the transition to the labour market can be quite marked, with "selective" systems producing a limited output of graduates who are expected to move into specific openings (and the supply may be very strictly controlled), while more accessible systems yield a large number of completers, who are then expected to compete for the available positions.

Streaming or tracking of students into certain programmes and courses may differ between nations. One country may attempt to sort, stream or channel students early in their education into technical, vocational or terminal programmes that link with particular kinds of job, while another country may provide little or no streaming, leaving the private sector to train workers. The extent to which the private sector is involved in education and training, both formally and informally, will also influence the relationship between education and work. In some countries, business invests heavily in its workers; in others, education and training are conducted mainly through the formal public or private education systems.

Part of the belief systems referred to above may involve different approaches to financing post-secondary education. Under the open-access model, it may be the case that advanced education is regarded as a social or public good which is financed largely out of general tax revenues. On the other hand, an "elite" model may include the assumption that since there is a large individual gain realised by the few who attend, they should pay a substantial part of the cost. Different beliefs about the collective versus individual benefits of education and access to education will condition transition.

The extent to which parents and the general public *support* education, both in terms of money and time, will make a difference to school functioning. Some countries may have a tradition of public involvement in education (by parents, volunteers, business and labour organisations, and local communities), which makes education relevant and connected to its stakeholders, while in other countries there may be less direct support, and education may be less well related to the practical, applied issues of the day.

There may also be variation in public satisfaction with education, and in the public's expectations of education systems, both in general terms, and of specific aspects. In one country, satisfaction with education may be low, particularly with the connection or lack of a connection with jobs, employment and incomes. The education system may be regarded as too detached, abstract and theoretical. It may also be seen as too broad and child-centred. In another country, the concern may be that the education system focuses too much on technical training for labour markets, and is too narrow and authoritarian. In the latter country, there may be a view that education should be broadened to provide a general or liberal education, whereas opinion in the former country will tend in the opposite direction.

Countries also differ in the extent to which they stress certain areas of study, and attempt to channel students into these. Some encourage students to choose specific fields of study which may be considered important to their economic development, such as mathematics and science programmes, and discourage enrolment in more general fields, such as the humanities and the arts, while others take a less interventionist approach. Different interpretations are possible when the absolute numbers enrolled in mathematics and science programmes are used in statistics, rather than percentages of the total population.

In some jurisdictions, transitions between school and work have been described as a "market", or a "trial-and-error" approach. That is, students make crucial *choices* of education and programme, and then compete in unconstrained labour markets. There is no formal involvement in the transition process on the part of educational institutions or employers. The signals sent by employers to students are vague and general, and the signals received by students are confused and may offer little incentive or motivation for school work which focuses on achieving the knowledge or skills required by specific industries.

In contrast, in other jurisdictions an "institutional" approach is taken, which is characterised by organised interactions between institutions such as firms, schools, unions and governments, which serve to guide and support individuals as they make the transition from education to careers, and in some cases to manage the transition and select the individuals involved. Under the institutional model, there is formal involvement by educational institutions and employers in the transition process, and the signals sent by employers and received by students are clear and precise. Different approaches will produce very different transitions.

Finally, there are major differences among countries in terms of how they handle social *mobility*. There are permeable class structures, in which open competition and achievement determine the eventual place in the social order; and there are more closed class structures, in which mobility is largely determined by sponsorship or background. These pervasive differences condition not only selection, progress and outcomes of education, but also destinations and callings in the occupational structures.

## 7. Goals and Values

"The interpretation of indicators must be done in context, against the background of national goals and values – the figures cannot be permitted to 'speak for themselves' (Nuttall, 1992)."

National goals and values are important contextual determinants, particularly in an international environment where nations are seeking their niche or competitive advantage. Nations which are attempting to produce and provide very specific economic goods and services may structure their education systems in accordance with these economic plans, and this will lead to the creation of strategic national goals for education. If agreement can be reached within the country on those objectives, they can provide a focus for assessment and improvement of education. On the other hand, if the goals or objectives of the education system are vague or undefined or the ways of achieving them are unclear, "then no information is useful and anything or nothing will serve as an indicator" (OECD, 1973, p. 15). The experiences of students as they move from formal education to their first jobs will be affected by national goals and values.

## 8. Historical and Political Issues

Events in a country's past affect current political realities and have an impact on the functioning of education systems and labour markets. Some factors which contribute to these issues have already been touched upon in the earlier sections on demographic, geographical, economic and social factors, but others are specifically brought about by the political realities of the country. These realities may give rise to different degrees of authority being granted to central, regional or local levels of government. The sharing of authority may not be uniform across all policy areas. For instance, economic and trade issues may be controlled primarily by the central level, while education may be the responsibility of regional levels. The extent to which these differences in control exist will result in each jurisdiction adopting an education system which attempts to meet the needs of the country's population and economy, while perhaps not being directly involved in several other key aspects of human resource development. These factors may even extend beyond national boundaries, as trading blocks require member states to harmonise certain features of their education and labour markets in order to remove any factors which may be perceived as having a detrimental impact on the other members.

## 9. Conclusion

This chapter has only provided a brief sketch of some of the factors which have to be considered when the network indicators are used to compare educational outcomes in the labour market between one jurisdiction and another. These factors may have a direct impact on the inputs, process, and outcomes of the education system in a country. As a result, their impact may be relatively easy to understand and to take into consideration during the use of the indicator. However, they may also have indirect impacts and work in more subtle ways on whatever the indicator is trying to summarise. In these cases, that impact may be less obvious to the casual user, and care should be taken before conclusions about the advantages or disadvantages of certain approaches are drawn.

# References

NUTTALL, D. (1992), ''The functions and limitations of international educational indicators'', in OECD (Ed.), *The OECD International Education Indicators: A Framework for Analysis,* CERI, Paris.

OECD (1973), *Indicators of Performance of Educational Systems,* Paris.

OECD (1993), *Education at a Glance: OECD Indicators* (bilingual), 2nd edition, CERI, Paris.

# La transition entre l'école et l'emploi

## *Transition from school to employment*

*par*

**Michel-Henri Gensbittel**
Direction de l'évaluation et de la prospective
Ministère de l'Éducation nationale, Paris, France
*et*
**Christine Mainguet**
Service de Pédagogie expérimentale
Université de Liège, Liège, Belgique

Les conditions de transition entre l'école et l'emploi ont fortement évolué depuis les années 70. La frontière entre formation initiale et activité n'est plus aussi clairement tracée, en raison du développement des différents dispositifs destinés à faciliter l'accès à l'emploi, et comportant souvent une part de formation professionnelle. La croissance du chômage, la flexibilité dans la gestion de la main-d'œuvre, le recours accru aux emplois de durée limitée ont contribué à augmenter la durée d'accès à l'emploi stable. L'analyse de la transition professionnelle, qui est d'une importance capitale pour évaluer les politiques de formation professionnelle ou d'aide à l'insertion, doit tenir compte de ces évolutions. La comparaison internationale en ce domaine doit reposer sur la mise en perspective de nombreux indicateurs, afin de prendre en considération les différents contextes économiques et sociaux. Les éditions successives de *Regards sur l'éducation,* progressivement enrichies, donnent quelques éléments utiles, mais qui ne sont pas encore suffisants. Si le développement d'indicateurs composites tirés des sources statistiques usuelles est une piste qu'il faudra explorer plus avant, la généralisation d'enquêtes spécifiques ou de l'introduction de questions spécifiques dans les grandes enquêtes statistiques devrait être envisagée.

*

* *

# Summary

*The factors governing the transition from school to employment have markedly evolved since the 1970s. The boundary between initial training and participation in the labour force is no longer clearcut owing to the development of various schemes facilitating access to employment, which often include some vocational training. Rising unemployment, flexible labour management and the spreading practice of short-term jobs mean that it takes longer to gain access to stable employment. The analysis of vocational transition, which is a crucial factor in the evaluation of vocational training or insertion aid policies, must take these trends into account. In this field international comparison must be based on weighing many indicators together in order to take the various economic and social contexts into consideration. The successive editions of* Education at a Glance, *which are progressively expanding, supply useful information but this is still not sufficient. While the development of composite indicators culled from routine statistics is an approach that merits further exploration, more widespread use of specific surveys and the introduction of specific questions in major statistical surveys should be envisaged.*

\*

\*     \*

## 1. Le concept de transition

Jusque dans les années 70, la question de la transition entre l'école et la vie professionnelle ne se posait pas dans la plupart des pays. On s'intéressait certes aux relations entre formation et emploi, mais c'était d'abord dans le souci de mettre en place les formations nécessaires au développement des économies, qui nécessitaient une main-d'œuvre qualifiée de plus en plus nombreuse. L'objectif premier était l'estimation du nombre nécessaire de nouveaux diplômés. L'idée d'analyser le processus qui conduit de l'école au travail ne s'imposait pas : on pensait, et quelquefois on constatait, que la plupart des jeunes trouvaient rapidement un emploi à l'issue de leur formation initiale, à l'exception sans doute des moins qualifiés.

Le développement de la crise économique durant les années 70 n'a cependant pas épargné les jeunes débutants, de plus en plus nombreux à connaître le chômage. En parallèle, le discours qui consiste à faire porter la responsabilité des difficultés d'insertion des jeunes sur les dispositifs de formation s'est aussi fortement développé. L'inadéquation des formations initiales par rapport aux exigences du monde du travail est alors devenu un argument de plus en plus fréquemment cité. Les conditions étaient en quelque sorte réunies pour que l'on s'intéresse beaucoup plus directement au devenir des jeunes entre la fin de leur scolarité et leur accès à l'emploi «stable», afin de répondre aux préoccupations des pouvoirs publics : quels sont les facteurs facilitant une insertion professionnelle réussie ? Faut-il mettre en place des politiques spécifiques d'aide à l'accès à l'emploi ? Les formations professionnelles existantes sont-elles suffisantes ? Le processus de transition est alors devenu lui-même un objet d'analyse.

La notion de transition se réfère à un passage entre deux états distincts : la scolarité et l'emploi stable. Entre ces deux états peut s'écouler un laps de temps assez long, au cours duquel les jeunes peuvent passer par des périodes de chômage, bénéficier de dispositifs d'aide à l'insertion ou de formations complémentaires, avoir des emplois temporaires de courte durée ou à temps partiel, etc.

Au milieu des années 90, l'intérêt pour cette question n'a pas diminué, bien au contraire, mais les difficultés d'analyse grandissent. L'état initial et l'état final du processus de transition sont en effet de plus en plus difficiles à identifier et à dater.

Les formations en alternance, sous contrat de travail ou non, sont de plus en plus nombreuses et de statut parfois ambigu : s'agit-il d'abord d'un emploi ou d'abord d'une formation ? Même s'il existe un cadre juridique précis, les intéressés n'en ont pas toujours une conscience claire, et les enquêtes auprès des individus se heurtent à cette difficulté : elles ne peuvent qu'enregistrer l'appréciation (subjective) que les individus portent sur leur situation, privilégiant tantôt l'aspect formation, tantôt l'aspect emploi. En dehors de l'alternance, de nombreux jeunes occupent un emploi, souvent à temps partiel, en marge de leurs études ; c'est particulièrement le cas des étudiants : pour certains, il s'agit de financer en partie leurs études, pour d'autres, qui ont commencé à travailler, la reprise d'études permet plutôt d'obtenir un complément de formation. Par ailleurs, de nombreuses formations professionnelles dites «continues» s'adressent aussi aux jeunes sans emploi et sans qualification, et jouent en fait souvent le rôle d'une formation initiale. Enfin, il n'est pas rare de constater des reprises de formation initiale de type scolaire ou universitaire après un court passage sur le marché du travail. Il n'est pas facile dans ces conditions de définir précisément ce qu'est la fin de formation initiale.

Par ailleurs, la flexibilité qui caractérise la gestion de la main-d'œuvre dans les entreprises, la multiplication des formes d'emploi permettant aux employeurs d'obtenir une aide des pouvoirs publics pour une durée limitée et le recours fréquent aux contrats de courte durée sont quelques facteurs, parmi d'autres, qui rendent difficile tout jugement sur la stabilité des emplois occupés par les jeunes débutants.

Si dans ce contexte une analyse du processus qui mène de l'école à l'emploi reste pertinente, les indicateurs à construire devront être désormais plus complexes, et les jugements plus nuancés.

## 2. Les enjeux politiques de l'analyse de la transition entre l'école et l'emploi

L'analyse de la transition entre l'école et l'emploi peut être réalisée dans le but d'évaluer les résultats des politiques de formation initiale. L'insertion professionnelle des jeunes au terme de la scolarisation initiale est en effet un des principaux objectifs poursuivis par les systèmes éducatifs. Le cadre de référence des indicateurs INES place de ce fait les données sur la transition entre l'école et l'emploi parmi les indicateurs de résultats, au même titre que les indicateurs relatifs aux acquis des élèves ou aux diplômes obtenus.

La collecte d'informations sur les conditions d'insertion des jeunes peut déboucher sur une réorganisation de l'offre de formation. L'interrogation de cohortes de sortants peut permettre également d'améliorer les procédures d'orientation des jeunes pendant leur cursus scolaire. Cette orientation scolaire et professionnelle est un élément important de l'organisation pédagogique des systèmes éducatifs et les initiatives visant à l'améliorer prennent des formes diverses selon les pays : éducation des choix professionnels reconnue comme élément du curriculum de base, intervention de professionnels, soit au sein de l'école, soit en dehors, etc.

Les enquêtes de cheminement (enquêtes longitudinales), par la mise en évidence des trajectoires professionnelles, fournissent des éléments d'évaluation des mesures prises par les pouvoirs publics pour faciliter l'accès des jeunes à l'emploi (par exemple en offrant aux jeunes chômeurs une formation professionnelle continue ou des stages d'aide à la recherche d'un emploi). Il est fréquent de constater que des jeunes bénéficient successivement de plusieurs de ces mesures, et seule une analyse longitudinale permet de juger de l'efficience des politiques mises en œuvre. Cette méthode permet aussi de mesurer empiriquement les effets des incitations financières à l'embauche des jeunes (diminution des charges patronales, diminution du salaire minimum garanti, etc.). Il est aussi possible, dès que le champ de l'enquête est assez vaste, de mettre en évidence la concurrence entre les catégories de jeunes suivant le niveau et le type de formation suivie (formation générale ou professionnelle, dans un établissement scolaire ou en alternance par exemple).

Enfin, si les coûts économiques liés à ces politiques doivent être analysés en fonction de leur efficacité, les coûts sociaux résultant des difficultés rencontrées par les jeunes au cours de cette phase de transition doivent aussi être pris en considération. L'analyse des trajectoires individuelles doit en particulier permettre d'identifier, dans un contexte où on constate une élévation nette du niveau de formation des jeunes, des processus de marginalisation menant certaines catégories d'entre eux au chômage de longue durée et au sous-emploi. Les coûts économiques de ces phénomènes et les problèmes sociaux qu'ils entraînent peuvent être considérables à long terme.


## 3. Les facteurs influant sur la transition entre l'école et l'emploi

Dans le domaine de la transition professionnelle, il faut se garder de comparaisons trop directes entre pays, à partir de critères simples. De nombreux facteurs, longuement présentés dans le chapitre 4 de cet ouvrage, se combinent et pèsent inégalement selon les pays, au sein de modèles sociétaux différents. Les conditions de la transition entre l'école et l'emploi ne peuvent pas uniquement s'interpréter en termes économiques, par exemple d'investissement rationnel en capital humain : elles dépendent aussi de caractéristiques plus globales, comme les modalités de la formation initiale, l'équilibre entre générations, la place des jeunes dans la société et dans les embauches, l'importance accordée à la formation pour accéder à l'emploi par les différents groupes sociaux, etc.

De ces nombreux facteurs, on ne rappellera ici que les principaux. Au premier rang, on relève bien entendu l'organisation des systèmes éducatifs et plus particulièrement l'impact de caractéristiques comme l'âge de fin de scolarité obligatoire, le développement plus ou moins important de filières de courte durée conduisant à des qualifications professionnelles reconnues, la part des formations techniques ou professionnelles initiales par rapport aux formations générales, etc. Par exemple, la faible extension de la formation professionnelle initiale au sein du système scolaire (au Japon entre autre) en fait reporter le poids sur les entreprises, et engendre des conditions tout à fait particulière d'accès à l'emploi.

Les taux de scolarisation dans le secondaire supérieur ou les taux d'accès à l'enseignement supérieur sont le reflet de l'utilisation par les jeunes des différentes possibilités offertes par le système : la diversité dans l'offre et la demande de formation induit des taux d'activité juvéniles très variables selon les pays. Les taux de diplômés aux différents niveaux permettent *a contrario* d'estimer les sorties sans diplômes, phénomène encore très fréquent dans certains pays. Dans la plupart des cas, une majorité de jeunes entament leur vie professionnelle avec un diplôme de niveau secondaire. La part des jeunes diplômés de l'enseignement supérieur parmi ceux qui chaque année entrent sur le marché du travail varie fortement selon les pays.

D'une façon générale, la formation reçue (durée, type, niveau, etc.) et l'ensemble du curriculum sont des éléments importants qui vont jouer sur le processus d'insertion. D'autres conditions du déroulement de la scolarité doivent aussi être prises en compte : les stages de formation en entreprise, les formations en apprentissage, l'exercice d'un emploi pendant la scolarité ont souvent une influence positive sur l'insertion professionnelle ultérieure, même si elle n'est parfois qu'indirecte.

Parmi les autres caractéristiques des systèmes éducatifs qui influent sur la transition entre l'école et l'emploi, il faut signaler également les possibilités d'éducation et de formation au-delà de la scolarisation initiale. Ces formations dites parfois de la seconde chance permettent à des jeunes qui ont quitté le système scolaire sans qualification de reprendre des études, parfois d'obtenir un diplôme, et d'améliorer ainsi leurs chances d'insertion professionnelle.

La démographie peut expliquer la place faite aux jeunes sur le marché du travail : la pyramide des âges détermine en effet très largement l'importance du renouvellement de la main-d'œuvre, et donc les possibilités d'emploi pour les générations accédant à l'activité. Les possibilités d'accès des filles à l'emploi diffèrent de celles des garçons (voir chapitre 8).

La situation économique joue bien évidemment un rôle majeur dans l'insertion des jeunes. Mais on peut constater que, selon les pays, les ajustements imposés par les difficultés économiques pèsent inégalement sur les jeunes. Pour comprendre cette diversité, il est nécessaire d'analyser les politiques de gestion de la main-d'œuvre et de recrutement des entreprises. Celles-ci disposent en effet de nombreux moyens d'évolution : former mieux le personnel en place, recruter des salariés venant d'autres entreprises, recruter des chômeurs expérimentés, recruter des jeunes débutants dotés de diplômes élevés, recruter des jeunes peu diplômés qui seront formés peu à peu, faire appel à des apprentis, etc. La place des jeunes débutants dans l'ensemble des mouvements de main-d'œuvre dépend de ces politiques d'embauche, dont les caractères dominants diffèrent selon les pays (Elbaum et Marchand, 1993; Lefresne, 1994; Rault, 1994). On constate dans certains pays une nette préférence pour la main-d'œuvre expérimentée (en France par exemple), alors que d'autres se caractérisent par un investissement élevé des entreprises dans la formation professionnelle des jeunes (l'Allemagne par exemple).

Certaines entreprises, certains pays, ont par ailleurs des politiques très marquées de flexibilité et de recours aux emplois de courte durée : on peut ainsi observer dans certains cas un accès rapide à l'emploi, facilité par l'existence d'un *turn-over* élevé, mais avec une probabilité élevée de retombée ultérieure au chômage. Certains secteurs économiques, certaines catégories d'emploi ou d'entreprises sont à l'inverse difficiles d'accès, mais leur gestion de main-d'œuvre, si elle allonge considérablement le délai d'obtention d'un emploi, rend plus improbable le retour au chômage.

Les facteurs liés aux individus sont également très importants. L'origine sociale et le milieu familial peuvent aider à trouver un emploi : un capital social et culturel hérité des parents est souvent un avantage, mais les jeunes peuvent aussi bénéficier d'un réseau de relations (en particulier professionnelles) de parents en activité; autant d'avantages dont sont privés les jeunes issus de milieux défavorisés, dont les parents sont eux-mêmes souvent au chômage.

## 4. Les indicateurs disponibles sur la transition entre l'école et l'emploi

A partir de la deuxième édition de *Regards sur l'éducation* (OCDE, 1993), le Réseau B a proposé des indicateurs relatifs à la période de fin de la scolarité et de début de la vie active.

Dans un premier temps, les données classiques telles que le taux de chômage des 15 à 24 ans (par sexe) ou la part des jeunes actifs et des jeunes chômeurs dans la population âgée de 15 à 24 ans (indicateur C6 dans la deuxième édition de *Regards sur l'éducation)* ont été complétées par des taux d'activité par niveau de diplôme dans la tranche d'âge supérieure, les 25 à 34 ans (annexe S7 dans la deuxième édition de *Regards sur l'éducation*).

Ces premières informations étaient encore fort sommaires. Construites en prenant comme référence une tranche d'âge (et non un âge de sortie du système scolaire), elles ne permettaient pas de tirer des conclusions sur le processus de transition entre l'école et la vie active. Tout au plus pouvait-on constater, chez les jeunes, des taux de chômage élevés, mais fort variables selon les pays, et observer qu'un taux d'activité faible ne s'accompagnait pas nécessairement d'un taux de chômage bas.

D'après le relevé établi par les membres du Réseau B, peu de pays mènent régulièrement des enquêtes d'insertion sociale et professionnelle (moins d'un an après la fin des études) ou des enquêtes longitudinales de cheminement (cinq ans après la fin des études). Ces enquêtes sont bien souvent partielles (un type de diplôme, une région seulement, etc.) et non récurrentes. La taille des échantillons, le taux de couverture et les méthodologies sont très variées. Dans certains cas, l'enquête porte sur l'ensemble des sortants; ailleurs seuls les diplômés sont interrogés, etc. Elles se déroulent à des moments différents selon les pays, les périodes de référence et les durées d'observation sont variables (un an, deux ans, voire cinq ans après la sortie des études). Il s'agit de cohortes tantôt suivies régulièrement, tantôt d'enquêtes rétrospectives. Ainsi, en l'absence de systèmes exhaustifs d'enquêtes régulièrement répétées, il est difficile de disposer, pour les mêmes années, de données décrivant à court et moyen terme le devenir des sortants de formation initiale. Cependant, dans la troisième version de *Regards sur l'éducation* (OCDE, 1995), il a été possible de présenter l'indicateur R24, calculé à partir d'enquêtes nationales. Le Réseau B a décidé, dans un premier temps, de ne publier que les taux de chômage des sortants de formation initiale, un an et cinq ans après la fin de leur scolarité, par niveau CITE. Les résultats disponibles sont présentés de façon synthétique au tableau 5.1.

Les données relatives à l'Allemagne, disponibles mais trop anciennes, n'ont pas été retenues dans la publication. Des informations sur les taux d'activité ont également été collectées, mais il a également été jugé préférable de ne pas les publier pour l'instant (ce point est discuté plus loin). Enfin, les années de référence ne sont pas les mêmes selon les pays et les niveaux, et les méthodologies diffèrent (cohortes interrogées plusieurs fois, assemblage de plusieurs enquêtes, etc.).

Les données disponibles et publiées ne permettent donc pas encore facilement une comparaison entre pays. En particulier, le calcul du rapport du taux de chômage des sortants au taux de chômage de différents groupes d'âge dans l'ensemble de la population active n'a pas été publié. S'il n'est pas possible d'effectuer dès maintenant ce type de calculs, on peut cependant juger de l'intérêt qu'ils auront, en faisant avec la plus grande

Tableau/Table 5.1.

**Taux de chômage des sortants par niveau CITE**

*Unemployment rate for school leavers by ISCED level*

| | Secondaire inférieur CITE 2 | | Secondaire supérieur CITE 3 | | Supérieur court CITE 5 | | Supérieur long CITE 6/7 | |
|---|---|---|---|---|---|---|---|---|
| | 1 an | 5 ans | 1 an | 5 ans | 1 an | 5 ans | 1 an | 5 ans |
| Australie | 33 | – | – | – | – | – | – | – |
| Canada | – | – | – | – | 8 | 8 | 9 | 6 |
| Danemark | 9 | 23 | 15 | 12 | 11 | 5 | 12 | 6 |
| Espagne | 34 | 34 | 36 | 21 | 13 | 7 | 26 | 13 |
| Finlande | 18 | 17 | 10 | 6 | 3 | 2 | 1 | 1 |
| France | 57 | 34 | 24 | 18 | 8 | 4 | 12 | 5 |
| Irlande | 35 | – | 24 | – | 21 | – | 10 | – |
| Italie | – | – | – | – | – | – | 39 | – |
| Royaume-Uni | 15 | – | 13 | – | – | – | – | – |
| Suède | 8 | 16 | 13 | 5 | – | – | – | 3 |
| Suisse | – | – | – | – | 12 | – | 8 | 3 |
| États-Unis | 37 | – | 12 | – | 6 | – | 8 | – |

*Source :* OCDE (1995), Indicateur R24.

Tableau/Table 5.2.

**Taux de chômage par groupes d'âge**

*Rate of unemployment by age group*

| | Groupes d'âge | | | |
| --- | --- | --- | --- | --- |
| | 15-24 ans | 25-34 ans | 45-54 ans | 25-64 ans |
| Allemagne | 5 | 6 | 6 | 6 |
| Australie | 18 | 10 | 7 | 9 |
| Canada | 18 | 12 | 8 | 10 |
| Danemark | 11 | 14 | 9 | 11 |
| Espagne | 34 | 21 | 10 | 15 |
| États-Unis | 14 | 8 | 6 | 7 |
| Finlande | 23 | 13 | 10 | 11 |
| France | 21 | 11 | 7 | 9 |
| Irlande | 23 | 15 | 12 | 14 |
| Italie | 33 | 14 | 4 | 7 |
| Royaume-Uni | 15 | 10 | 7 | 8 |
| Suède | 11 | 6 | 2 | 4 |
| Suisse | 6 | 3 | 2 | 3 |

*Source :* OCDE (1995), Indicateur R21.

prudence la simple juxtaposition des taux de chômage par groupes d'âge, pour les seuls pays concernés (tableau 5.2).

Même si les taux de chômage des plus jeunes ne sont parfois calculés que sur une faible population (quand les taux de scolarisation sont élevés), il est visible que le chômage frappe inégalement les différentes générations dans la plupart des pays. Le prix payé par les jeunes semble ainsi relativement élevé en Espagne, en France ou en Italie, par exemple, alors que le poids du chômage semble mieux réparti sur les différents groupes d'âge au Danemark ou en Allemagne (qui a été rajoutée dans ce tableau en raison de sa situation extrême). Le rapprochement entre les taux d'activité et de chômage et les données portant sur les jeunes sortants semble donc prometteur : on peut par exemple noter dans certains pays une sorte de préférence de la part des employeurs, à niveau de formation égal, pour des travailleurs expérimentés, conduisant à un processus d'insertion long et difficile pour les jeunes débutants et à des taux de scolarisation élevés, et donc à des taux d'activité faibles et des taux de chômage élevés chez les jeunes.

Les différences relevées suscitent toutefois quelques réflexions. Ce chapitre porte sur la transition entre l'école et l'emploi. Mais, comme on l'a souligné, les frontières de ce que nous appelons l'école, de façon générique, ne sont pas toujours clairement tracées. Il existe, dans de nombreux pays, des dispositifs de formation professionnelle (sans contrat de travail) ou de compléments de formation générale, destinés aux jeunes sortis du système scolaire formel sans qualification. Selon que ces dispositifs sont comptés ou non comme faisant partie de la formation initiale, le champ de l'indicateur R24 (au moins pour le niveau CITE 2, correspondant au secondaire inférieur) n'est pas le même, et les taux d'activité diffèrent. On constate dans certains pays des taux d'activité très faibles un an après une sortie de formation au niveau CITE 2, qui pourraient être dus à la prise en charge de certains jeunes par des dispositifs spécifiques, non comptés dans le système éducatif.

La même question peut être posée à propos de l'apprentissage, tantôt considéré comme une formation, tantôt comme un emploi. Des taux de chômage particulièrement faibles pourraient s'expliquer si les apprentis sont comptés comme en emploi *parmi les sortants*. Il sera donc certainement nécessaire de préciser la définition des sortants, présentée en détail dans le chapitre 3, afin de lever ces incertitudes : délimitation homogène dans tous les pays de ce que l'on retient comme formation initiale au sein de tous les dispositifs de formation existants (système scolaire formel, apprentissage, autres dispositifs, etc.), inclusion des diplômés comme des non-diplômés dans le champ des enquêtes. Les enquêtes existantes ne permettront cependant peut-être pas cette harmonisation. Dans certains pays, elles sont en effet organisées avec le concours des établissements scolaires traditionnels, qui sont facilement identifiables : l'extension de ces enquêtes aux sortants d'organismes de formation plus divers pourrait poser des problèmes pratiques d'organisation.

Enfin, il sera nécessaire de s'assurer que le service militaire est comptabilisé de la même façon dans tous les pays : les jeunes effectuant leur service militaire ont souvent été, par le passé, considérés comme inactifs, alors que les normes internationales imposent maintenant de les considérer comme ayant un emploi. Ces différences de méthode peuvent expliquer certaines variations des taux d'activité ou de chômage, et fausser les comparaisons internationales.

Si des enquêtes d'insertion et de cheminement devenaient plus fréquentes, et si les méthodologies étaient harmonisées, il serait possible de les exploiter pour calculer d'autres indicateurs comparables internationalement, déjà disponibles pour certains pays, sur le processus d'insertion : par exemple, la durée avant d'accéder à un emploi stable ou le pourcentage de jeunes qui connaissent plus d'une année de chômage, par sexe, par grandes filières.

## 5.   Les indicateurs en cours de développement

En plus de l'indicateur R24, dont le développement est en cours, plusieurs projets doivent être mentionnés.

Les conditions dans lesquelles se déroule la formation doivent pouvoir être prises en compte dans l'analyse de la transition entre l'école et l'emploi. Des systèmes très divers de formation initiale existent actuellement dans les différents pays de l'OCDE. Des modes de formation, courants dans certains pays, sont en passe d'être adoptés par d'autres. Dans bien des cas, les partenaires éducatifs s'efforcent de collaborer de manière plus active avec les futurs employeurs des élèves. Une évaluation plus précise devrait être menée de l'impact de dispositifs tels que l'alternance, les stages en entreprise, etc., sur l'insertion professionnelle des jeunes qui en bénéficient. Le Réseau B a rédigé un projet d'indicateur sur ce thème, mais qui n'a pas encore été développé.

Un point plus particulier de la vie scolaire devrait être envisagé avec plus de précision dans le cadre de l'analyse de la transition professionnelle : il s'agit du phénomène des étudiants/travailleurs. Une des conséquences de l'allongement de la période de transition semble en effet être le développement du travail étudiant qui peut prendre des formes diverses. Les sources actuelles des indicateurs du Réseau B (recensement, enquêtes sur la population active) pourraient fournir une première estimation de ces comportements dans les différents pays Membres, à condition que des réponses qui, *a priori*, s'excluent (inactivité et emploi) soient admises dans les questionnaires.

Parmi les facteurs extérieurs au système scolaire, la démographie est abordée dans *Regards sur l'éducation* (1992 et 1993) par la part des jeunes dans la population totale. L'indicateur est actuellement présenté selon un découpage par tranches d'âges (5-14, 15-24, 25-29 ans). Pour pouvoir être exploité dans le cadre d'une analyse de la transition professionnelle, il devrait être affiné par la mise en évidence de la part des jeunes en âge d'être actifs (les 15-29 ans) dans le total des actifs (les 15-64 ans).

Les modes de gestion de la main-d'œuvre des entreprises des différents secteurs sont encore mal connus. Un indicateur est en projet dans le réseau sur les sources de recrutement. Il devrait être calculé à partir d'enquêtes comparables réalisées auprès d'employeurs dans les divers pays Membres. Il devrait permettre d'identifier les professions, les secteurs d'activité ou les catégories d'entreprises accueillant les jeunes débutants, et de connaître les types de formation qui y sont privilégiés.

Enfin, l'analyse de la transition entre l'école et l'emploi devrait faire intervenir également un indicateur sur les formations professionnelles suivies en dehors du système scolaire par les jeunes qui n'ont pas connu une insertion directe ou satisfaisante dans le marché du travail. L'indicateur sur l'éducation des adultes proposé par le réseau pour la troisième édition de *Regards sur l'éducation* (OCDE, 1995) devrait pouvoir être proposé pour la tranche d'âge des 15 à 24 ans, à condition que la définition des frontières de la formation initiale ait pu être précisée, comme on l'a indiqué plus haut. Il semble toutefois difficile d'isoler, dans les sources statistiques usuelles, les formations destinées aux jeunes chômeurs, puisque ceux-ci sont habituellement comptés comme inactifs dès lors qu'ils commencent une formation. Leur décompte n'est envisageable que grâce à des sources administratives, par exemple quand leur formation est financée par les pouvoirs publics.

Au-delà de ces indicateurs, dont le rôle est d'apporter des éléments explicatifs sur l'insertion des jeunes, d'autres projets d'indicateurs portant spécifiquement sur la transition entre école et emploi sont à l'étude.

Dès le début de la troisième phase du projet INES, le Réseau B a discuté d'un indicateur qui fournirait une mesure relative et non plus absolue, de la difficulté d'insertion que connaissent les jeunes actuellement. Dans la proposition initiale, chaque pays était invité à rassembler le plus de données possibles sur les jeunes (par exemple les 15-24 ans) qui cherchent à s'insérer professionnellement : le type d'emploi obtenu, le type de contrat, les qualifications requises, le salaire, les avantages sociaux auxquels ils ont droit, etc., afin de calculer un score composite d'insertion, propre au pays. Pour chaque catégorie de diplômés on calculerait ainsi un score moyen qui serait référé à la moyenne nationale pour l'ensemble des jeunes. L'indicateur international serait basé sur les écarts observés, par catégories de diplômés, par rapport à la moyenne «nationale». Ce genre de calcul offre l'avantage de tenir sous contrôle beaucoup des paramètres clés qui ont été cités, et qui rendent difficiles par ailleurs dans la plupart des cas la comparaison internationale.

Les premières expérimentations menées en France à partir de l'enquête sur la population active montrent que l'on obtient aisément un score composite décrivant correctement les conditions d'insertion professionnelle et sociale de différentes catégories de jeunes. La limitation à la tranche des 15-24 ans exclut toutefois une part trop importante des jeunes ayant suivi des études supérieures. Cependant, si on élargit le calcul à une tranche d'âge plus large, il reste difficile de contrôler les effets de l'ancienneté inégale sur le marché du travail : un jeune de 25 ans peut avoir quitté le système éducatif depuis 8 ou 9 ans, un autre du même âge peut avoir quitté l'université avec un diplôme d'enseignement supérieur depuis quelques mois. Enfin la comparaison internationale des écarts entre les sous-populations les plus favorisées et les moins favorisées suppose la construction de scores ayant une distribution normale centrée réduite (Loi de Laplace Gauss). Cette condition n'est pas facile à remplir sans utiliser des techniques statistiques spécifiques. Les travaux méthodologiques devront donc continuer sur ce point.

D'autres indicateurs en projet dans le réseau ont pu connaître un début d'expérimentation, pour essayer de remédier au faible nombre d'enquêtes longitudinales disponibles. Ainsi, à partir de données de stock (recensement), une tentative a été faite pour calculer le taux de chômage, par niveau d'études, des personnes ayant terminé leur formation initiale un an ou cinq ans avant la date de référence, en prenant comme référence non pas l'âge mais l'ancienneté dans la recherche d'emploi. Ce type de calcul n'est possible que si l'on connaît l'année de fin d'études. Cette information, qui demanderait une définition très rigoureuse, est très peu souvent demandée dans les enquêtes utilisées actuellement, ou bien d'une fiabilité incertaine.

Un dernier projet du Réseau B concerne un indicateur qui mettrait en évidence une adéquation/inadéquation entre formation initiale et emploi. Il n'est pas question de proposer d'estimer, dans des comparaisons internationales, une quelconque relation mécanique, terme à terme, entre une filière de formation et une profession. Le projet fait plutôt référence à une observation plus précise des débouchés professionnels, à l'issue d'une même formation, afin d'estimer la diversité et la qualité des emplois occupés. Un des objectifs serait par exemple de mesurer, de manière comparable dans les pays OCDE, l'ampleur de la sur-qualification de certains jeunes qui prennent un emploi dans des postes subalternes.

Il faut enfin mentionner que l'OCDE a, sous le titre de «Itinéraires et participation dans l'enseignement technique et la formation professionnelle» (VOTEC), lancé une importante réflexion sur le développement de l'enseignement professionnel et technologique (OCDE, 1994). On trouve dans ce programme des points communs avec les préoccupations du Réseau B à propos de la transition entre l'école et l'emploi : où se trouve la frontière entre formation initiale et formation continue, quel est le poids des itinéraires ou des filières de formation, quels sont les facteurs d'attraction ou de rejet à l'égard de l'enseignement professionnel et technologique ? L'état du marché du travail, les salaires offerts, les conditions de travail et les possibilités de promotion sont des données importantes dans cette approche. Le Réseau B ne pourra donc que bénéficier dans un proche avenir de ce programme de travail de l'OCDE.

## 6.  Priorités pour le développement de futurs indicateurs

Les réflexions qui précèdent plaident pour une meilleure concertation entre les fournisseurs et les utilisateurs des statistiques existantes. Dès à présent, dans *Regards sur l'éducation*, des données statistiques sur les flux de sorties de l'enseignement sont mises en rapport avec les résultats des enquêtes de cheminement et des enquêtes sur la population active. Il a toutefois été souligné à plusieurs reprises qu'un effort d'harmonisation et de précision dans la définition de certains concepts ou catégories statistiques reste nécessaire au sein du Réseau B (*cf.* chapitre 3).

Il est également nécessaire d'obtenir des informations complémentaires. Ces informations peuvent provenir d'une exploitation différente (selon d'autres ventilations par exemple) de données existantes de façon à en tirer le maximum. Le calcul de nouveaux ratios, la mise au point d'indicateurs composites doivent faire l'objet de nouvelles recherches.

Mais les travaux du Réseau B permettent ou permettront aussi d'identifier les modifications marginales aux enquêtes statistiques existantes que l'on pourrait préconiser, ou d'indiquer les enquêtes qu'il serait utile de généraliser en partant d'expériences nationales convaincantes.

L'existence, par exemple, de questions permettant de connaître la date de fin de la formation initiale et la date d'obtention du dernier diplôme des personnes de moins de 35 ans dans les recensements ou les enquêtes sur la force de travail serait d'une grande utilité.

Il serait souhaitable par ailleurs de parvenir, à moyen terme, à la réalisation régulière d'enquêtes longitudinales, menées auprès des sortants de formation initiale sur une base méthodologique commune dans tous les pays concernés. Dans cette perspective, plusieurs partenaires doivent être associés au processus de collecte des données. Parmi eux, les institutions scolaires ou universitaires devraient jouer un rôle majeur en collaborant de manière active à la phase de collecte auprès de leurs anciens élèves et étudiants, qu'ils aient ou non mené leur formation à terme. Toutes les catégories de diplômés devraient être couvertes dans l'analyse, de l'enseignement supérieur à la formation professionnelle initiale.

Enfin, il est important de souligner la nécessité de disposer de données récurrentes, obtenues à intervalles réguliers qui permettront, à terme, de mesurer l'évolution conjoncturelle.

# Références

ELBAUM, M. et MARCHAND, O. (1993), «Emploi et chômage des jeunes dans les pays industrialisés : la spécificité française», *Premières synthèses*, DARES, ministère du Travail, de l'Emploi et de la Formation professionnelle, n° 34, Paris, octobre.

LEFRESNE, F. (1994), «Europe, disparités des marchés du travail», *Chronique internationale*, IRES, n° 24, Noisy-le-Grand, mai.

OCDE (1993), *Regards sur l'éducation : les indicateurs de l'OCDE* (bilingue), 2e édition, CERI, Paris.

OCDE (1994), «Itinéraires et participation dans l'enseignement technique et la formation professionnelle (VOTEC)», document, Paris.

OCDE (1995), *Regards sur l'éducation : les indicateurs de l'OCDE,* 3e édition, CERI, Paris.

RAULT, C. (1994), *La formation professionnelle initiale, contrastes et similitudes en France et en Europe*, La documentation française, Paris.

# Education, Employment and Unemployment

## *Formation, emploi et chômage*

*by*

**Birgitte Bovin**
Ministry of Education, Copenhagen, Denmark

Questions of supply and demand in the labour market are closely related to the effort to increase productivity and enhance the competitive position of the OECD countries. Education is an important theme in the debate about unemployment in the OECD countries. The higher the level of educational attainment of the population, the lower the level of unemployment and the higher the labour force participation rate tend to be. However, the question is asked as to the role of education in combating unemployment. Some countries with high levels of educational attainment also experience high levels of unemployment. The labour force participation rate co-varies with the level of educational attainment: that is, persons holding a university degree tend much more often to be in the labour force than persons having completed less than upper secondary education. The latter are also more often unemployed.

Network B has developed and presented three main indicators on education, employment and unemployment. They relate to a number of other education indicators, such as general level of educational attainment of the population, labour force participation rates, transition characteristics, costs of education, and the distribution of earnings from work by levels of educational attainment. Forthcoming indicators on this theme may refer to active labour market policies and specific programmes for the young unemployed.

\*

\*     \*

## Note de synthèse

*Ce chapitre entend montrer que les indicateurs mis au point par le Réseau B peuvent servir à analyser la relation entre formation et emploi. L'auteur formule certaines conclusions provisoires, mais signale aussi qu'il est difficile d'utiliser les informations données par les indicateurs pour effectuer des comparaisons internationales. Il en conclut qu'il n'est pas possible de parvenir à des réponses définitives et qu'un complément d'information est nécessaire. Il suggère plusieurs domaines qui demandent des informations plus complètes. Il définit en outre des thèmes de travaux futurs, comme les programmes spéciaux en faveur des jeunes chômeurs et les prévisions de l'offre et de la demande de main-d'œuvre.*

*Les indicateurs internationaux doivent permettre de déterminer la situation d'un pays par rapport à une caractéristique importante. Le Réseau B a mis au point et présenté des indicateurs qui montrent quelle est la situation d'un pays quant au niveau de formation et au taux de chômage, par exemple. Mais les indicateurs ne renseignent pas seulement sur le niveau de formation ou le taux de chômage dans un pays par rapport à d'autres, ils aident aussi à comprendre les relations qui existent entre ces indicateurs. Quatre relations sont analysées dans ce chapitre.*

*Premièrement, existe-t-il une relation entre le niveau général de formation et le taux de chômage lorsqu'on les compare d'un pays à un autre ? Deuxièmement, un niveau de formation donné se traduit-il par le même taux d'activité dans les différents pays ? Troisièmement, y-a-t-il une relation entre un faible chômage et une forte activité chez des individus ayant un niveau de formation différent ? Enfin, la répartition de l'emploi et du chômage est-elle la même selon le niveau de formation, le sexe et l'âge dans les différents pays ?*

*Ce chapitre constate que plus le niveau de formation est élevé, plus le taux de chômage est faible. Toutefois, cette conclusion ne signifie pas nécessairement que développer la formation est un moyen efficace de lutter contre le chômage car plusieurs pays Membres de l'OCDE ont à la fois un taux de chômage élevé et une main-d'œuvre dûment formée. En outre, il est à noter que le taux d'activité varie d'un pays Membre de l'OCDE à l'autre en fonction du niveau général de formation. Les indicateurs mis au point par le Réseau B montrent aussi, d'une manière générale, que la répartition de l'emploi et du chômage n'est pas la même selon le niveau de formation, le sexe et l'âge.*

\*

\*    \*

## 1. Introduction

In the 1990s, unemployment affects all groups in society. In 1995, 35 million people in the OECD countries – 8.5 per cent of the labour force – are estimated to be out of work, and at least a quarter of them are young people who have recently left the initial education and training system.

Education is an important variable in labour market analysis. In general, there is apparently a close relationship between the level of educational attainment and the risk of unemployment. Nonetheless, interpretation of indicators on the labour market outcomes of education is not as unambiguous as it may seem to be. Rumberger (1994) notes, for instance that:

"There is a substantial body of empirical and theoretical research that demonstrates a powerful linkage between educational outputs and a variety of economic and social outcomes. However, the linkage is less straightforward and more complex than commonly perceived. Thus, it is very difficult to determine accurately the extent to which educational outputs are contributing to economic and social outcomes as opposed to other factors. In particular, since economic outcomes result, at least in part, from the operation of the labour market and the interaction of supply and demand, changes in the supply characteristics of the population in the form of their educational qualifications can have no predetermined impact on economic and social outcomes (Rumberger, 1994, p. 282)."

Despite this, output indicators on education, employment and unemployment can be used to monitor some key components of the education and labour market systems and can help to determine the extent to which the two systems are aligned.

From the perspectives of both labour market policy and education policy, there is a need to reflect on the linkages between different policy areas. Many key questions can be asked from a cross-sectorial point of view. For example, should countries rely on regular courses of education for young people, or should priority be given to lifelong education and continuing vocational training for adults? Should countries organise special programmes in order to support groups that are marginalised or at risk? Should they take a short-term or a long-term view? Which is more economically viable, and which is right from a political, ethical and moral perspective? How can education help to optimise a country's educational competitiveness? The general experience is that it is difficult to predict and to counter shortages of labour and mismatches of skills, or other obstacles in the labour market.

At the national level, statistics and indicators on unemployment, broken down according to levels of education, are of obvious importance to politicians, legislators and administrators, given that national policy seeks to correct imbalances between labour demand and supply and, more generally, to overcome rigidities. Therefore, despite the difficulty of making accurate predictions, great efforts are often made to document and analyses imbalances, and to understand their possible economic and social consequences. International education indicators can assist in this effort.

The experience gained in Network B demonstrates that it is relevant to compare indicators of education and labour market conditions in the OECD countries. It is possible to do so, although the difficulty of doing justice to country-specific conditions should not be underestimated. The experience of Network B shows that it has been possible to obtain data from most countries, although problems of definition and reliability remain.

Network B's interest in developing international indicators on education and the labour market is not unique. In its annual publication *Employment Outlook,* the OECD regularly presents statistical information on employment and educational attainment, often focusing on long-term unemployment. However, the Network B indicators tend to include more countries and use the accepted international classification of education, ISCED. The indicators developed by Network B are clearly and explicitly grounded in educational statistics.


## 2. Three Key Indicators


In the third edition of *Education at a Glance* (OECD, 1995), there are three indicators which give a broad description of the relationships between education, employment and unemployment. Two of them (C11 and C12) are classified as input indicators showing the economic and social context in which education systems operate, while the third (R21) is considered an outcome indicator:

- *Labour Force Participation Rate by Educational Attainment* (C11): the labour force participation rate is related to the educational structure. In aggregate, the structure and frequency of unemployment also depend on this.
- *Unemployment Rates by Gender and Age* (C12): this indicator shows whether lack of education has a particularly negative effect on the employment of specific groups. It can also be interpreted as an outcome indicator with a focus on similarities and dissimilarities between generations and genders in acquiring education and finding work.
- *Unemployment Rates by Educational Attainment* (R21): this indicator shows whether lack of education in general may be associated with unfavourable employment conditions in OECD countries. It also indicates the magnitude of differences in the unemployment rate at different levels of education. The indicator shows, for example, whether a long-cycle tertiary education is an equally good guarantee against unemployment in all the countries.

The indicators on educational attainment (C11) and unemployment (R21) have been included in the series of indicators from the start of Network B. It may be argued that they do not provide much new information in relation to what is generally known. However, they contribute significantly to the understanding of other indicators, for instance, educational expenditure, participation rates and entry ratios. Moreover, an important reason for continuing to include these indicators is that many countries do not normally produce statistics on employment and unemployment for all levels of education, as is currently done for the INES project. In labour force statistics there is, on the other hand, a strong tradition of relating employment and unemployment to variables such as professional affiliation, union membership or unemployment insurance funds. When education is included in the analysis, it is most often dealt with in terms of the level of educational attainment for specific occupational groups, such as teachers, nurses or engineers.

# 3. Results

Network B indicators may be used to shed light on questions such as:

- Is there a relationship between the level of educational attainment and the level of unemployment across countries?
- Does a given level of educational attainment co-vary with the level of labour force participation in different countries?
- Is there a relationship between low unemployment and high labour force participation for persons at the different levels of education?
- Are employment and unemployment distributed in the same way according to education, gender and age in different countries?

So far, Network B has been able to confirm that there is a significant spread in the general, officially registered unemployment rate between OECD countries. The OECD average for 1991 was 6.8 per cent, varying between countries from 1.4 per cent to 13.6 per cent.

In Table 6.1, the national unemployment rates for different levels of education have been divided by the country rate for ISCED level 3 and expressed as indices with 100 as a base. Through this transformation, the differences between countries are eliminated and it becomes easier to compare the relative unemployment rate at different levels of educational attainment across countries. The column on the right in Table 6.1 shows the unweighted overall unemployment rates.

At the lowest level of education (ISCED 0/1/2), the average index for all countries is 150, *i.e.* 50 per cent higher than the country rate for level 3. All countries except Italy, Switzerland and Turkey are above 100; Finland, Portugal, Spain and Sweden, however, are not much above. For tertiary education (ISCED 5 and 6/7) the indices vary around 50-70, but with Switzerland (low general rate) as an exception at the university level and Australia at the non-university level. In most countries, however, the unemployment indices decrease in a regular way from the lowest to the highest level. Thus, the country profiles support the hypothesis that education tends to counteract unemployment.

The linkage between education and unemployment is complex and depends on many individual, societal and economic preconditions. In times of oversupply of labour in relation to market demands, employers tend to choose persons with higher qualifications. The uneven distribution of unemployment by education may also result from the greater flexibility of persons with a tertiary education qualification. An important factor behind these differences is that the number of jobs for people with a low level of education is tending to decrease in the OECD countries. More of the available jobs require a higher level of educational attainment than was the case in the 1980s.

In 1993, the average unemployment rate in the OECD countries had increased to 7.8 per cent, while the uneven educational distribution remained. This points to the possibility of an increasing polarisation between those with the lowest and those with the highest level of educational attainment (see Table 6.2). Also, persons with an upper secondary education as their highest level of educational attainment have a relatively high unemployment rate.

Table/Tableau 6.1.

**Relative unemployment rate by level of educational attainment in the workforce
25 to 64 years of age, 1991**

(rate for upper secondary education = 100)

*Taux de chômage relatif par niveau de formation de la population active
âgée de 25 à 64 ans en 1991*

(taux pour un niveau d'enseignement secondaire du 2ᵉ cycle = 100)

| | Early childhood, primary and lower secondary education ISCED 0/1/2 | Upper secondary education ISCED 3 | Tertiary education, short duration ISCED 5 | Tertiary education, long duration ISCED 6/7 | Unemployment rate, average for all ISCED levels |
|---|---|---|---|---|---|
| North America | | | | | |
| Canada | 149 | 100 | 82 | 54 | 9.1 |
| United States | 190 | 100 | 70 | 44 | 6.8 |
| Pacific Area | | | | | |
| Australia | 151 | 100 | 109 | 69 | 7.1 |
| New Zealand | 148 | 100 | 72 | 56 | 8.1 |
| European Community | | | | | |
| Belgium | 278 | 100 | 55 | 39 | 7.8 |
| Denmark | 156 | 100 | 63 | 51 | 9.9 |
| France | 161 | 100 | 55 | 57 | 7.8 |
| Germany | 159 | 100 | 70 | 68 | 6.6 |
| Ireland | 277 | 100 | 67 | 47 | 13.6 |
| Italy | 80 | 100 | – | 70 | 6.1 |
| Netherlands | 177 | 100 | 82 | 77 | 6.1 |
| Portugal | 126 | 100 | 29 | 57 | 3.8 |
| Spain | 112 | 100 | – | 76 | 12.9 |
| United Kingdom | 160 | 100 | 56 | 48 | 7.1 |
| Other Europe-OECD | | | | | |
| Austria | 155 | 100 | – | 48 | 3.4 |
| Finland | 124 | 100 | 41 | 30 | 6.6 |
| Norway | 152 | 100 | 53 | 36 | 4.1 |
| Sweden | 113 | 100 | 49 | 50 | 2.1 |
| Switzerland | 89 | 100 | 57 | 151 | 1.4 |
| Turkey | 79 | 100 | – | 43 | 5.7 |
| OECD mean | 150 | 100 | 63 | 56 | 6.8 |

*Source:* National data submissions.

Among people with a low level of educational attainment in particular, the proportion of long-term unemployed is greater than among people with a high level of educational attainment (OECD, 1993*a*, p. 91 and 1994*a*, p. 23). The incidence of unemployment tends to rise for any given level of educational attainment.

In Table 6.3, data collected by Network B for *The OECD Jobs Study* (OECD, 1994*b*) show variations in the rate of long-term unemployment among all unemployed persons. Some of the differences reflect different total unemployment levels and a number of different standards and definitions (p. 26). The magnitudes differ widely

Table/Tableau 6.2.

## Relative unemployment rate by level of educational attainment in the workforce 25 to 64 years of age, 1981 and 1992

(rate for upper secondary education = 100)

### *Taux de chômage relatif par niveau de formation de la population active âgée de 25 à 64 ans en 1981 et 1992*

(taux pour un niveau d'enseignement secondaire du 2ᵉ cycle = 100)

| | Year | Early childhood and primary education ISCED 0/1 | Lower secondary education ISCED 2 | Upper secondary education ISCED 3 | Tertiary education, short duration ISCED 5 | Tertiary education, long duration ISCED 6/7 | Unemployment rate, average for all ISCED levels |
|---|---|---|---|---|---|---|---|
| **North America** | | | | | | | |
| Canada | 1981 | 156 | 144 | 100 | 81 | 54 | 5.6 |
| | 1992 | 160 | 155 | 100 | 92 | 54 | 10 |
| United States | 1981 | 158 | 153 | 100 | 69 | 37 | 5.8 |
| | 1992 | 183 | 190 | 100 | 64 | 40 | 6.6 |
| **Pacific Area** | | | | | | | |
| New Zealand | 1981 | 158 | 101 | 100 | 95 | 94 | 2.3 |
| | 1992 | 175 | 87 | 100 | 61 | 49 | 8 |
| **European Community** | | | | | | | |
| Denmark | 1981 | – | 155 | 100 | 68 | 38 | 6.3 |
| | 1992 | – | 170 | 100 | 63 | 52 | 10.6 |
| France | 1981 | 126 | 159 | 100 | 68 | 68 | 5.6 |
| | 1992 | 146 | 180 | 100 | 63 | 60 | 8.8 |
| Spain | 1981 | 110 | 110 | 100 | – | 58 | 8.2 |
| | 1992 | 109 | 125 | 100 | 89 | 70 | 14.7 |
| United Kingdom | 1984 | – | 150 | 100 | 54 | 47 | 8.5 |
| | 1992 | – | 176 | 100 | 40 | 44 | 8.4 |
| **Other Europe-OECD** | | | | | | | |
| Finland | 1982 | – | 140 | 100 | – | – | 3.7 |
| | 1991 | – | 123 | 100 | 47 | 28 | 11.4 |
| Norway | 1981 | 104 | 191 | 100 | 55 | 64 | 1.3 |
| | 1992 | 145 | 145 | 100 | 57 | 37 | 4.6 |
| Sweden | 1991 | 147 | 194 | 100 | 38 | 38 | 2.2 |
| | 1992 | – | 108 | 100 | 53 | 47 | 3.8 |

*Source:* National data submissions.

between countries, and the interpretation is not clear. However, the figures show less variation between levels of education than expected. In many countries, a relatively high percentage of the long-term unemployed have gained a tertiary education qualification.

A high level of educational attainment in the population is often accompanied by a high labour force participation rate. The average labour force participation rate for different educational groups varies from 64 to 91 per cent. Table 6.4 examines the labour force participation rates of the population which has attained at least upper secondary education (ISCED 3 and above). In general, there is a positive correlation between these

Table/Tableau 6.3.

**People who have been unemployed one year or more as a percentage of all unemployed by level of educational attainment, 1992**

*Personnes au chômage pendant un an ou plus en pourcentage du total des chômeurs par niveau de formation, 1992*

| | Early childhood and primary education ISCED 0/1 | Lower secondary education ISCED 2 | Upper secondary education ISCED 3 | Tertiary education, short duration ISCED 5 | Tertiary education, long duration ISCED 6/7 | Total |
|---|---|---|---|---|---|---|
| North America | | | | | | |
| Canada | 17 | 15 | 13 | 12 | 11 | 14 |
| United States | 11 | 14 | 13 | 15 | 13 | 13 |
| Pacific Area | | | | | | |
| Australia | – | 49 | 45 | 41 | 33 | 46 |
| New Zealand | 54 | 45 | 43 | 39 | 25 | 47 |
| European Community | | | | | | |
| Denmark | – | 37 | 33 | 30 | 33 | 35 |
| France | 51 | 37 | 32 | 20 | 28 | 37 |
| Germany | – | 47 | 35 | 30 | 32 | 37 |
| Spain | 48 | 53 | 57 | 25 | 39 | 51 |
| United Kingdom | – | 50 | 34 | 28 | 30 | 40 |
| Other Europe-OECD | | | | | | |
| Finland | – | 12 | 6 | 0 | 0 | 8 |
| Norway | 62 | 38 | 31 | 29 | 35 | 33 |
| Sweden | – | 14 | 8 | 10 | 9 | 10 |
| Switzerland | – | 27 | 21 | 29 | 17 | 23 |

*Source:* National data submissions.

measures, but there are countries with a relatively high level of educational attainment that have a relatively low labour force participation rate. The explanation might be found in demographic conditions, such as the age composition of the population.

Women who have completed long-cycle tertiary education programmes tend to have a relatively high labour force participation rate in all countries – almost at the same level as that of men. The differences between the countries are small. Women with a low level of educational attainment have a relatively low labour force participation rate, but for this group it varies markedly from one country to another. Evidently, the higher the level of educational attainment, the greater the similarity between men's and women's participation in the labour market and the greater the similarity between countries (*cf.* Chapter 8).

The labour force participation rate among young people (15-24 years of age) also varies significantly. The rate, of course, depends on the proportion of young people who are still enrolled in education and on their opportunity of finding a job. There are marked differences in youth unemployment in relation to the general unemployment level of the

Table/Tableau 6.4.

**Percentage of the population having attained at least upper secondary education and relative rate of labour force participation by level of educational attainment in the workforce 25 to 64 years of age, 1992**
(participation rate for people with upper secondary education = 100)

*Pourcentage de la population ayant terminé au moins le 2ᵉ cycle de l'enseignement secondaire et taux d'activité relatif par niveau de formation de la population active âgée de 25 à 64 ans, 1992*
(taux d'activité des personnes ayant terminé le 2ᵉ cycle de l'enseignement secondaire = 100)

| | Rate of the total population with at least upper secondary education | Participation in labour force rate | | | |
|---|---|---|---|---|---|
| | | Total population 25-64 years of age | Upper secondary education ISCED 3 | Tertiary education, short duration ISCED 5 | Tertiary education, long duration ISCED 6/7 |
| **North America** | | | | | |
| Canada | 71 | 78 | 100 | 107 | 112 |
| United States | 83 | 79 | 100 | 109 | 111 |
| **Pacific Area** | | | | | |
| Australia | 53 | 74 | 100 | 104 | 111 |
| New Zealand | 56 | 75 | 100 | 102 | 113 |
| **European Community** | | | | | |
| Belgium | 45 | 68 | 100 | 108 | 113 |
| Denmark | 59 | 83 | 100 | 105 | 105 |
| France | 52 | 75 | 100 | 107 | 104 |
| Germany | 82 | 76 | 100 | 113 | 117 |
| Ireland | 42 | 65 | 100 | 116 | 124 |
| Italy | 28 | 65 | 100 | – | 114 |
| Netherlands | 58 | 70 | 100 | – | 111 |
| Portugal | 14 | 69 | 100 | 103 | 108 |
| Spain | 23 | 64 | 100 | 111 | 108 |
| United Kingdom | 68 | 78 | 100 | 103 | 110 |
| **Other Europe-OECD** | | | | | |
| Austria | 68 | 68 | 100 | – | 120 |
| Finland | 62 | 80 | 100 | 101 | 108 |
| Norway | 79 | 81 | 100 | 107 | 112 |
| Sweden | 70 | 91 | 100 | 101 | 102 |
| Switzerland | 81 | 82 | 100 | 112 | 113 |
| Turkey | 14 | 61 | 100 | – | 121 |
| **OECD mean** | 55 | 78 | 100 | 108 | 112 |

*Source:* OECD (1995), Indicators C01 and C11.

countries (OECD, 1994*a*, p. 22). In some countries, young people bear a relatively large part of unemployment. In the same countries it is, moreover, relatively common that young people do not register for work in the labour market. Finally, a common phenomenon in some countries is the existence of special programmes for young people who may encounter – or are already experiencing – difficulties in finding work. Such programmes will affect the statistics on youth unemployment. Similar active labour market pro-grammes, with the same effect on the rates, exist also for older people.

The association between educational attainment and labour force participation seems remarkably similar throughout the OECD countries. In Table 6.4, the labour force participation rates for different levels of education have been divided by the country rate for ISCED level 3 and expressed as indices with 100 as a base. The indexed figures confirm that in all countries except Australia, the participation rates increase in a regular way from ISCED 3 to ISCED 6/7. Graduates of tertiary education programmes will in almost all cases register for work in the labour market. However, whether they find a job which corresponds to their educational qualifications is another matter. For many years and in many countries, there has not been an unambiguous relationship between the specific content of the education and the job actually obtained. However, students acquire, in addition to specialised competence, a number of more general qualifications which can be widely used in the labour market. There are, of course, different cultural, social and economic patterns in the OECD countries, but the basic relationships between education, employment and unemployment seem to be identical. The indicators produced by INES Network B can tell whether the level and distribution of education and unem-ployment in a country are low relative to the patterns observed in other, comparable countries.

## 4.   Related indicators

Indicators on education, employment and unemployment cannot and must not be seen in isolation. In the INES project, there are a number of related indicators which, together with the three mentioned above, provide a framework for understanding the information on inputs, processes and outcomes that is offered by other indicators. Such related indicators are, for instance:

- *Level of Educational Attainment of the Population* (C01): this indicator increases the understanding of the demographic and educational composition of the entire population.
- *Transition from Secondary to Tertiary Education* (P04): this indicator gives addi-tional information about investment in tertiary education, and the extent to which it is a guarantee against unemployment. The results tend to show that university education does not offer a sufficient guarantee against unemployment, but that it certainly improves employment prospects.
- *Participation in Formal Education* (P01): this indicator provides information about the number of young people who are enrolled in education, and about the distribution by levels of education. It reflects the general educational effort of the countries, and the assignment of priorities between, for instance, secondary and tertiary education. To effect a substantial change in the educational profile of the population will, however, take many years.
- *Educational Attainment of Workers in Specific Occupations and Industries* (R23): this indicator provides additional information on the national labour markets of the countries and on the links between education and types of job.

- *Education and Earnings* (R22): this indicator has been discussed and refined since the start of Network B. Together with the indicators on education, employment and unemployment, it provides important information on the incentives for investment in education and the individual returns (see also Chapter 7).

Network B has discussed, defined and to some extent adopted other indicators, which broadly speaking lie within the domain of education, employment and unemployment. Some have been abandoned because of a lack of appropriate data, while others which are included in the network's programme of work must be further elaborated (*cf.* Chapter 2).

## 5. Some Weaknesses and Possible Improvements

The indicators in the second edition of *Education at a Glance* (OECD, 1993*b*) generally refer to rather broad levels of education. For instance, ISCED 3 (upper secondary education) is not always divided into general and vocational programmes, and ISCED levels 5, 6 and 7 (tertiary education) are often presented as one level, or as two levels by combining 6 and 7. The indicators offer valuable but condensed information.

The lack of distinction between general and vocational education programmes may make the information less relevant in some cases, in particular in a labour market context. Furthermore, for all levels from ISCED 3 upwards, there is much variability within each level. Within university education, for example, there is a great variation, between physicians with low unemployment and architects with high unemployment.

It would be of great value if more background information about the labour market structures of the OECD countries could be incorporated into the project. It would then be easier to interpret the results, if they could be compared, for instance, in the light of the national distribution according to size of businesses, occupations and industries. Such additional information is important because the supply and demand of persons with specific educational qualifications are to a large extent influenced by the labour market structures of the countries.

Finally, indicators on education, employment and unemployment could with advantage be used for labour market forecasting. Both education and labour market statistics are traditionally used for such forecasts. The data collected by the network could be fruitfully employed in a forward-looking manner.

## 6. Summary

The purpose of international indicators is to provide knowledge about where a country stands nationally, and they should make ready comparisons with other countries possible. Network B has developed and presented indicators which show the relationships between education, employment and unemployment.

Unemployment is an important theme in the OECD countries. The question is, however, whether education can be used as a means of combating unemployment. Or, alternatively, does the educational structure contribute to creating unemployment? What about the long time it takes to change the qualification level of the labour force through improved education of the young, and through continuing education and training for those already in the labour force? These questions are touched upon in this chapter, which takes as its point of departure three indicators on unemployment and labour force participation rates distributed by levels of educational attainment, gender and age. The three indicators show the outcomes of the education system as well as the economic and social context in which the education system operates.

International indicators on education and the labour market reflect considerable variations in the levels of unemployment and educational attainment between countries. In general, however, there is a strong relationship between the unemployment rate and educational attainment. The incidence of unemployment tends to fall for any given level of education from ISCED 1/2 to 6/7.

The data confirm that education is one instrument, among others, for countering rising unemployment, but its effect is more long-term than short-term. Within the OECD there are countries whose population has reached a high level of educational attainment, but which nevertheless experience high general unemployment rates. A relatively high percentage of the unemployment in the same countries is estimated to be structurally conditioned due to problems of adaptation to new labour market structures and economic conditions. Thus it is more flexibility in the education system and the labour market, and not primarily higher levels of education, that is the objective. Nonetheless, it is important that young people should benefit from a sound and often lengthy education, because it is difficult to do anything about inadequate initial education later on in life. Besides, because of the magnitude of the problems and the generally declining number of young people in the labour market, continuing education and training should be given high priority in the 1990s.

Indicators on education, employment and unemployment relate to a number of other education indicators, such as the level of educational attainment of the entire population, the costs of education, the distribution of earnings by levels of education, participation rates, and transition characteristics. Forthcoming indicators on this theme may refer to special programmes for the young unemployed and to forecasts of supply and demand in the labour market.

# References

OECD (1992), *Employment Outlook*, Paris, July.

OECD (1993*a*), *Employment Outlook*, Paris, July.

OECD (1993*b*), *Education at a Glance: OECD Indicators* (bilingual), 2nd edition, CERI, Paris.

OECD (1994*a*), *Employment Outlook*, Paris, July.

OECD (1994*b*), *The OECD Jobs Study. Facts, Analysis, Strategies*, Paris.

OECD (1995), *Education at a Glance: OECD Indicators*, 3rd edition, CERI, Paris.

RUMBERGER, R.W. (1994), "Labour market outcomes as indicators of educational perform-ance", in A.C. Tuijnman and N. Bottani (Eds.), *Making Education Count: Developing and Using International Indicators,* OECD/CERI, Paris.

# The Rate of Return to Education: A Proposal for an Indicator

## *Le taux de rendement de la formation: proposition d'indicateur*

*by*

**Nabeel Alsalam**
National Center for Education Statistics, US Department of Education,
Washington, DC, United States
*and*
**Ronald Conley**
Pelavin Research Institute, Washington, DC, United States

Individuals decide how much education to pursue, in part, on the basis of the costs and the expected increase in earnings. Costs, in particular, are affected by governments' decisions on spending at each level of education and by government policies on tuition charges and financial aid. The internal rate of return is an indicator of the incentive for individuals to pursue further education and for the government to encourage them to do so. Both social and private rates of return may be calculated. However, social rates of return are most relevant to public decision-making. Among the limitations of these estimates are imprecision in the data and the inability to measure many benefits of education. Data that are a part of the OECD INES database were used to calculate rates of return to completing successively higher levels of education in ten Member countries. These data show that the increased earnings resulting from increasing levels of education are, in almost every case, substantially greater than the additional costs that are incurred. Estimates of the rates of return to different levels of education in OECD countries could be further improved if additional information for persons under age 25 were collected.

\*

\*      \*

## Note de synthèse

*Le propos de ce chapitre est de déterminer si un indicateur du taux de rendement interne serait utile pour l'élaboration de la politique gouvernementale et de montrer comment un tel indicateur pourrait être mis au point par le Réseau B du projet INES.*

*Le taux de rendement interne indique ce qui incite les individus à suivre une formation complémentaire et ce qui incite les pouvoirs publics à les y encourager. On peut calculer les taux de rendement aussi bien pour la société que pour les individus. Toutefois, les taux de rendement à l'échelle de la société intéressent plus directement les pouvoir publics. Quant aux individus, ils décident du niveau des études qu'ils comptent poursuivre en fonction notamment des coûts prévus de la formation envisagée et des avantages qu'ils comptent en retirer sous la forme de gains plus élevés. Les coûts, en particulier, dépendent des dépenses que les pouvoirs publics décident de consacrer à chaque niveau d'enseignement et des politiques gouvernementales en matière de droits d'inscription et d'aide financière.*

*Ce chapitre montre aussi comment les données recueillies par le Réseau B ont servi à calculer le taux de rendement interne d'études complètes d'un niveau de plus en plus élevé dans dix pays Membres. D'après les estimations, les gains accrus résultant d'une formation plus poussée sont, dans la plupart des cas, bien plus élevés que les dépenses supplémentaires engagées à ce titre.*

*Ce chapitre signale également les limites de l'indicateur que constituerait le taux de rendement interne de l'investissement consacré à la formation. Parmi les inconvénients signalés, on notera le fait que les données sur les coûts sont incomplètes, que les données sur les salaires sont imprécises et qu'il est impossible d'évaluer tous les avantages externes qu'offre une formation ou ses effets bénéfiques sur la consommation. Ce chapitre suggère un certain nombre de domaines dans lesquels des améliorations peuvent être apportées. Par exemple, les estimations du taux de rendement interne correspondant à différents niveaux de formation dans les pays Membres de l'OCDE seraient sans doute plus fiables si les données sur les salaires étaient établies par groupe d'âge à intervalles de cinq ans et si l'on pouvait obtenir des informations complémentaires sur les personnes de moins de 25 ans. Par ailleurs, il serait nécessaire de calculer des estimations distinctes des dépenses d'éducation par niveau de la CITE et de recueillir des données sur les variations du taux de rendement de l'enseignement.*

\*

\* \*

## 1. Introduction

A critical policy issue for national and regional governments is how to determine the appropriate expenditure level for the education of children and adults. Increasing the level of education of the population has many benefits, both to the individuals receiving education and to the nation. Among these benefits are the following:

- Raising levels of education may lead to an increase in national economic output because productivity levels among workers depend heavily upon the skills and knowledge acquired as a direct result of their formal education, or as a result of subsequent training which depends upon skills acquired in school. In addition, persons who are more highly educated tend to have a greater probability of gainful employment than persons with less education (Gelderblom and de Koning, 1994; Jorgenson and Fraumeni, 1989).
- Improving the educational levels of workers is one of the more effective ways of reducing the prevalence of poverty or dependence on government assistance because the earnings received by workers are, in large part, dependent upon their ability to contribute to the output of an enterprise. Blau and his colleagues (1988) observe that the World Bank has "strongly advocated increased investment in schooling in order to reduce inequality in earnings and income distributions in developing economies".

There are many other important benefits to be gained from improving the educational attainment of a country. The two just identified are those, however, that are the most frequently analysed for purposes of public policy. These benefits do not, however, indicate that nations should necessarily seek to maximise the educational attainments of their citizens. There are three important constraints on the expansion of educational services:

- There are major costs associated with increasing educational services. In 1991, in the twelve OECD countries providing information on the cost of education, total direct public and private expenditures came to 6.4 per cent of the combined Gross Domestic Products (GDP) of these countries. The percentage of GDP devoted to direct educational expenditures ranged from 5.0 per cent to 7.4 per cent (OECD, 1993, p. 66). These percentages substantially underestimate the actual national cost of education since they do not take account of the foregone earnings of students, and often represent incomplete measures of private educational expenses.
- Allocations of resources for educational purposes must compete with other important and beneficial uses of scarce resources, e.g. medical care, housing and other necessities of life, and child care.
- Finally, as resources for the provision of education are increased, the benefits of additional spending, both private and social, tend to decline. This phenomenon of diminishing returns has been frequently noted in the international literature on rates of return to education (e.g. Psacharopoulos, 1993). Schultz (1988) observes that "the social rates of return in some developing countries may be insufficient to warrant further expansion of subsidised higher education".

National and regional governments must take decisions, not only on the total amount of education to be supported, but also on the areas in which this support should be provided. For example, should emphasis be placed on guaranteeing all children access to a minimum level of schooling, or should more resources be allocated to higher education in order to assure a country of a continuing supply of individuals who are qualified to manage and develop technologically sophisticated enterprises? Levin (1989) cites studies of the cost-effectiveness of lengthening the school day, and using computers as instructional aids. Card and Krueger (1992) discuss the effects on the returns to education of raising teachers' pay and reducing classroom size.

Government decisions on the amount and composition of Khandker educational expenditures are based on: 1) the perceptions of policy-makers as to the benefits to be derived from these expenditures; and 2) resource constraints. It is important to emphasise that the decisions that must be made do not depend solely upon calculations as to whether overall educational expenditures are worthwhile. For all practical purposes, all countries have recognised the tangible and intangible benefits of providing educational programmes. Instead, countries make decisions whether to *increase* (or decrease) educational expenditures and in what areas. Economists use the term "marginal" to describe changes in programme levels, and the resulting benefits and costs of these changes are termed marginal benefits and marginal costs.

Because of difficulties in measuring many of the benefits of educational programmes, an exact comparison of benefits with the costs of education is not feasible. However, analysts frequently estimate one major benefit of education, increased earnings, and compare these increased earnings with the costs. Although there are several ways in which benefits can be compared to costs, a common approach in education is to calculate the *internal rate of return*.

The easiest way to conceptualise the internal rate of return is as an *average annual rate of return on investment*. Consider a deposit made in a savings account with a fixed rate of interest. That rate of interest is the internal rate of return on that savings account.

In principle, as long as the internal rate of return on investments in education exceeds internal rates of return on alternative expenditures, then increased investment is warranted. Because of diminishing returns, additional expenditures should cause the increased earnings of persons receiving the education to decline, causing the rate of return to decline, eventually reaching the point where additional expenditures are not warranted.

The estimated rates of return to education discussed in this chapter should be interpreted as estimates of the average return to individuals for completing the next level of education. From a public policy perspective, this is the return to creating more seats or financing higher enrolment in education. The results do not address the question of returns to improving the quality of the education that is provided.

## 2. Individual and Social Rates of Return

Although the basic principles are relatively straightforward, many conceptual and empirical issues are encountered in calculating rates of return on educational expenditures.

## Distribution of Benefits and Costs

One issue results from the way in which the benefits and costs of schooling are distributed among different groups. We must distinguish between three categories of costs:

- *Direct resource use*, *e.g.* teachers' salaries, tutors' stipends, books and other supplies, school building depreciation, and rent, heat, electricity, etc.;
- *Foregone earnings*, *i.e.* the earnings lost by students while attending classes; and
- *Transfer payments*, *i.e.* payments made to students to enable them to obtain food, shelter, clothing and other essential items while attending school.

These costs may be borne privately by the individual (including his or her family) or publicly by the governmental authority and the taxpayers who support it. Consider direct resource use: in most countries, the bulk of these costs are paid directly by the governmental authority through tax-supported funds, B. However, individuals may purchase books and other supplies, and sometimes pay tuition to the school, A. It is the sum of these individual and government expenditures that represents total social outlays on resources for educational purposes, A+B.

Foregone earnings are also a major element of cost, particularly as students become teenagers and enter into their early twenties. However, these costs, F, are not entirely borne by students as the public sector also loses the taxes, T, that would have been paid on these earnings. Thus, the total social cost due to foregone earnings, F, is divided into T and F-T. It is also worth noting that F represents not just the foregone earnings that would have been paid by employers to individuals, but also any fringe benefits (such as health and retirement insurance) that are not reflected in an employee's nominal wages.

Transfer payments, Tr, represent a real cost to taxpayers who must finance them, and a benefit to students who receive them. However, there is no net social cost. These expenditures are not regarded as competing with alternative uses of these resources since these students would still require food, clothing, and shelter, whether or not they attended school.

These cost elements can be summarised as shown in Table 7.1.

Table/Tableau 7.1.

**Cost elements**

*Éléments de coûts*

|  | Individual | Taxpayer | Social |
|---|---|---|---|
| Resources | A | B | A+B |
| Foregone earnings | F-T | T | F |
| Transfer | (–)Tr | Tr | – |

A similar matrix can be developed for the benefits of increased education. In particular, the increased earnings (including fringe benefits) due to increased education are partly received by taxpayers in the form of public tax receipts and possibly lower public transfer payments, while the worker receives the remainder. Consideration of the distribution of costs and benefits makes it apparent that three different types of rate of return calculation can be made:

- A private or *individual* (the terms may be used interchangeably) *rate of return* showing the returns per unit of cost incurred by individuals attending school and their families (returns are estimated by increased earnings, reduced by increases in tax liability and reductions in public support);
- A *taxpayer rate of return* showing the returns per unit of cost incurred by taxpayers (returns are measured by increased tax revenues and reduction in public support expenditures); and
- A *social rate of return* showing the rate of return per unit of social cost (returns are measured by the increase in gross earnings).

The returns to students and to taxpayers sum to gross earnings. St. John and Masten (1990) calculate the return to taxpayers of a public investment in student financial aid.

Most of the literature on the rate of return to education does not clearly distinguish between the private and social rates of return to education (although this distinction is common when evaluating other social programmes). The human capital literature, for example, generally omits consideration of direct expenditures on education, choosing to emphasise foregone earnings while students are in school. This methodological approach places the focus on the decision of individuals to spend more time out of the labour force so that they may spend more time in education. The justification for omitting consideration of direct expenditures is that they are small in comparison to foregone earnings. For some, such as younger students attending expensive private schools or colleges, the assumption may not be appropriate. The human capital literature also does not generally distinguish between before-tax and after-tax earnings, primarily because of data limitations. Some part of tax revenue is used to provide services that are enjoyed by the taxpayer and so properly should be included in private returns, but another part of tax revenue is given (through social programmes) to other less fortunate citizens and should be excluded from private returns.

From the standpoint of public policy, it is the social rate of return that is appropriate. However, as pointed out by Leslie and Brinkman (1993), and many others, the private rate of return and, thus, individual behaviour is heavily influenced by the level of public support of education. The social rate of return changes only in response to changes in the environment, including: 1) changes in the number of individuals at different levels of education; 2) changes in the demand for products that require workers with differing levels of education; and 3) changes in technology that alter the productivity of workers with differing levels of education.

## Marginal Rates of Return

As observed above, decisions about resource allocation should be based on comparisons of marginal costs and benefits, not average (or total) costs and benefits. Almost all estimates of rates of return to education are based on marginal values since they usually compare the increased costs of an additional level of schooling with the increased earnings that result.

However, these estimates are usually based on average costs and average benefits for all students who attain the next level of education. Suppose that consideration was being given to increasing the percentage of a country's youth who complete upper secondary education. The decision whether to do so should be based on the additional costs and additional benefits only of the students who would be affected by the policy, that is, those who would not otherwise complete upper secondary education. It is probable that the rate of return to these additional students will be lower than the average rate of return to all students who achieve this level of education.

## Problems in Estimating Rates of Return

There are numerous empirical obstacles to estimating rates of return in education (Griliches, 1977). A few examples are considered below.

### Missing Information

One of the biggest problems is that there are many ways in which increased education may raise the quality of the lives of the students, as well as other members of society, which are difficult or impossible to quantify and measure. Simply listing these various benefits would require numerous pages. However, the seven main categories of these benefits are as follows:

- There is an immense quantity of "home production" by parents, *e.g.* child care, management and care of the home, and home maintenance, which is not only presumed to be enhanced by education, but may confer benefits that reverberate through future generations. For example, improved care increases the likelihood that children will attend college and, in turn, will provide better care for their children.
- Population growth will usually decline and children will be better cared for (McMahon and Boediono, 1992; Woodhall, 1974).
- There are "consumption" benefits in that people's ability to enjoy their income is substantially enhanced, *e.g.* through the pleasure of reading or enjoyment of travel.
- There are presumed to be psychic benefits. For example, the higher the level of education, the more secure people feel about themselves.
- Economic growth will increase because of the use of more advanced technology (McMahon and Boediono, 1992; Mincer, 1989).
- Average levels of unemployment may decline as workers become more flexible and able to adapt to changes in the economy.

- Other benefits include reduced crime, more voluntary work, inventions that increase productivity, improved ability to budget and spend income, increased job security, and enhanced ability to learn new skills (Leslie and Brinkman, 1993).

Jorgenson and Fraumeni (1989) presented estimates that the non-market benefits of education are about twice the market benefits of education in the case of men, and about five times the market benefits of education for women. These non-market values were based on such variables as household work, human capital investment, travel, leisure, and maintenance. Schultz (1988) believed that the omission of non-market production and human capital's contribution to these forms of production is a more serious omission in the study of low-income countries than in the study of industrially advanced countries.

*Imprecision of Causal Relationships*

Even when some information on the benefits of education is available, there are usually difficulties in relating these data to the effects of educational attainments. The data most likely to be available are those showing the earnings of a population cohort at one level of education compared to another population cohort with a different level of education.

The difference in earnings, however, may not be wholly attributable to differences in educational levels. Individuals who achieve higher levels of education may be more talented to begin with, and would have had higher earnings even if they had not pursued higher levels of education. Many studies have attempted to isolate the effect of education on earnings from the effect of initial talents. These studies invariably find a smaller but nonetheless profitable rate of return to educational investment. Psacharopoulos and Woodhall (1985) and Leslie and Brinkman (1993) reported that natural ability counts for less than 20 per cent of the additional earnings of educated workers.

Alternatively, individuals may pursue a level of education that qualifies them for a type of work where their talents are *comparatively* better. Of course, no individual has an *absolute* advantage in all types of work. In fact, most individuals may only have a *comparative* advantage at some types of work. The implication of this is that the actual difference in average earnings between successive levels of education understates the true earnings benefits of acquiring additional education. People who continue their education beyond ISCED 3 to ISCED 6 would have earned less than those who left formal education at ISCED 3. Individuals both with and without higher levels of education have a comparative advantage in what they do (Willis and Rosen, 1979.)

Other factors may also affect differences between cohorts, *e.g.* greater work experience, or systematic discrimination against a particular socio-economic class. One study (Angrist and Krueger, 1991) even noted that the month of birth can affect school completion rates. Psacharopoulos (1992) pointed out how selection factors among countries cast doubt on comparisons of educational achievement among students who achieve a given level of education in these countries.

Blaug (1985) observed that economists and others are reluctant to base policy solely on rate of return estimates because of omitted benefits and imprecision in the data. One major reason for concern is that these estimates may be used for more than just convincing people that education programmes are worthwhile. They may also be used to help to determine resource allocation: for example, how should educational expenditures be divided between higher education, intermediate education, and lower education? Should higher education resources be concentrated on individuals who appear particularly likely to succeed, on the basis of test scores, or should all persons be given equal opportunity of higher education?

It is when decisions must be made how to allocate scarce educational resources among different groups of citizens that the inaccuracies and unmeasured benefits of educational programmes become particularly important. For example, the enormous rise in educational expenditures for children with severe disabilities is clearly not based on conventional rate-of-return analysis.

## Findings from International Comparisons of Rates of Return

There have been hundreds of studies of the rates of return to education in different countries throughout the world. In addition, there have been a number of analysts who have compared rates of return from different countries. Some important observations have been made.

To begin with, despite the limitations noted above, the evidence on the benefits of education are overwhelming. For example, Lorenz and Wagner (1990) compared the returns to schooling in twelve European countries using the Mincer human capital earnings function. The study concluded that earnings among citizens increased by 5.2 per cent per year for each additional year of schooling. Note that this method of calculating the internal rate of return requires several assumptions described by Mincer (1974), including the ability to ignore both the direct cost of education and the part-time earnings of students – the justification being that one roughly pays for the other. There was, however, considerable variation among countries and the range went from 2.8 per cent to 8.4 per cent per year of schooling. In addition to years of schooling, years of work experience contributed to differences in earnings among people. Generally, each year of experience increased earnings by about one-half the amount of a year of education.

In addition, one of the most consistent conclusions is that the social returns to primary education are higher than the social returns for completing higher levels of education (Psacharopoulos, 1993; Blaug, 1979) and it is, therefore, most efficient for developing countries to invest heavily in assuring basic literacy. For example, the ability to read and communicate enables farmers to adopt modern farming techniques and to choose among various types of seed, fertilisers, and conservation methods. The cost of primary education is much lower than higher education because there is little or no loss of earnings or productivity in sending children to primary school. Blaug (1979) and McMahon and Boediono (1991) observed that large salaries and almost free university education may have led to over-investment in university education in developing countries (*cf.* also Schultz, 1988).

It should be noted that this conclusion is based almost entirely on the increased earnings of persons receiving schooling. In the theory of competitive wage determination, only those effects that are captured by the employer, *i.e.* that affect the productivity of the firm, will be reflected in the earnings of workers with more schooling. These effects include the effects on the productivity of workers with less schooling: workers with more schooling may increase the productivity of workers with less schooling through training and mentoring activities. However, "externalities" such as effects on the economy as a whole or effects on all firms in the industry will not be reflected in the earnings of these workers.

Moreover, it is also frequently noted that private rates of return are consistently higher than social rates of return (Psacharopoulos, 1993). This is largely because private educational costs are usually far below the social costs of education because of the public subsidies given to education. It has also been reported that the level of public subsidy increases with the level of education (Psacharopoulos, 1993; Jallade, 1973), which means that the subsidy tends to be largest among individuals who are the most affluent in a society.

Another finding is that both social and private returns to education generally decline as a country's per capita income rises (Psacharopoulos, 1993). It is possible that this result is due to the economic principle that the (marginal) productivity of human capital will fall as its quantity increases and the quantity of physical capital and the state of technology do not change. However, it may also be due to the fact that the cost of financing education is higher in countries with low per capita income. For example, the government may not be able to finance from public funds very many seats with a high subsidy, and loans may not be as readily available to finance tuition, to purchase books, and to pay for basic living expenses. Also, families in less wealthy countries may value the labour or earnings potential of their teenage sons and daughters too much to allow them to pursue higher levels of education. When the cost of financing education is high, only those individuals who expect a high rate of return will invest in education. Those who expect a rate of return below the cost of financing, expressed as the available rate of interest for a loan to pay the cost, will not make the investment. The result is that the average internal rate of return to education will remain high.

A further finding is that the returns to education of women are higher than those of men (Psacharopoulos, 1993). This does not, of course, mean that the earnings of women are higher than those of men, but that the *increase* in earnings relative to the costs of increasing the level of education is greater. This probably also reflects a much greater increase in women's labour force participation rates, compared to men, as levels of education increase (Behrman and Deolalikar, 1988).

Also, in secondary education, the returns to academic education are higher than to vocational education, largely because the unit cost of vocational education is much higher than the unit cost of academic education (Psacharopoulos, 1993).

Finally, Psacharopoulos (1993) reports that the returns to those who work in the private (competitive) sector are higher than those in the public (non-competitive) sector, and that the returns in the self-employment (unregulated) sector of the economy are higher than in the dependent-employment sector. Differences in these levels of return are probably partly associated with differences in earnings that are compensating for differences in job security in these three sectors.

## 3. Experimental Rate of Return to Education Indicator

Published in the third edition of *Education at a Glance* (OECD, 1995) is a measure of the relationship between education and earnings. This indicator, numbered R22 in the most recent edition, shows the ratio of earnings of persons in three educational categories (ISCED 0/1/2, ISCED 5, and ISCED 6/7) to the earnings of persons who complete ISCED 3. These results are presented by gender and two age categories (25-34 and 45-64 years). As expected, the ratios indicate that earnings were higher for groups with higher levels of education, regardless of age and gender. These ratios are indicative of the incentive for individuals in each country to achieve higher levels of education.

This indicator has one major weakness. It is strictly an indicator of the earnings *benefit* of completing more schooling. It does not relate these earnings differentials to the costs of achieving the higher levels of education.

An estimate of the internal rate of return (IRR) per unit of cost to various levels of educational attainment is a more comprehensive indicator. It would compare the increase in lifetime earnings received by individuals with the cost they incur by foregoing earning while in school, and with public and private expenditures to provide the education.

Data submitted to the INES project by ten participating countries, along with several strong assumptions, have been used to make such calculations. The assumptions were necessary to fill in missing data. In particular, it was assumed 1) that the level of earnings of persons under age 25 could be interpolated from the earnings of persons aged 25 to 29; and 2) that the foregone earnings of students were approximately two-thirds of those of persons of the same age in the labour force whose educational attainment was at the next lower ISCED level. Both assumptions were necessary because the INES database does not contain information on the earnings of individuals below age 25. The IRRs were calculated by comparing the increased earnings and the increased costs associated with each successive ISCED level. For example, the difference in earnings between persons who completed tertiary education and those who completed secondary education was compared with the costs of tertiary education. The different steps and components are described in Annex 7.1.

The rate of return to each ISCED level is presented in Table 7.2. It is the discount rate, equivalent to an interest rate, that would make the increased earnings associated with each ISCED level equal to the increased social costs associated with completing that ISCED level. These estimates are illustrative of what could be calculated and included in the fourth edition of *Education at a Glance* with a moderate amount of additional data collected.

For seven of the ten countries, a rate of return was not calculated for completing ISCED 2. These countries did not provide earnings data for persons who completed only

Table / Tableau 7.2.

**Rates of return to education in selected OECD countries, by gender and ISCED level, 1992**

(in per cent)

*Taux de rendement de la formation dans certains pays de l'OCDE, par sexe et niveau de la CITE, 1992*

(en pourcentage)

| | Men | | | | Women | | | |
|---|---|---|---|---|---|---|---|---|
| | Lower secondary education ISCED 2 | Upper secondary education ISCED 3 | Tertiary education, short duration ISCED 5 | Tertiary education, long duration ISCED 6/7 | Lower secondary education ISCED 2 | Upper secondary education ISCED 3 | Tertiary education, short duration ISCED 5 | Tertiary education, long duration ISCED 6/7 |
| Belgium (1989) | – | 3.5 | 15.7 | 7.5 | – | 2.6 | 5.7 | 12.9 |
| Denmark | – | 11.4 | 3.8 | 10.9 | – | 11.2 | 3.6 | 8.2 |
| Finland | – | 7.6 | 12.8 | 15.1 | – | 5.9 | 13.6 | 14.4 |
| France | – | 5.9 | 17.6 | 15.9 | – | 9.2 | 18 | 11.9 |
| Germany | – | 11.3 | 16.5 | 13.9 | – | 7.1 | 6.7 | 9.3 |
| Netherlands (1989) | 8.8 | 11.2 | 6.9 | 9.9 | 9.5 | 15.4 | 1.7 | 7.6 |
| Spain (1991) | 11.2 | 10.4 | – | 10.8 | 13.5 | 9.8 | – | 12.9 |
| Sweden | – | 6.9 | 8.2 | 11.8 | – | 6 | 7.4 | 10 |
| Switzerland | – | 13.2 | 12.8 | 7.5 | – | 18 | 8.6 | 4.9 |
| United States | 10.8 | 19 | 10.5 | 12.9 | 5.1 | 18.6 | 12.5 | 12.2 |

the ISCED 1 level, possibly because for many years education has been compulsory through the ISCED 2 level. For the same reason, educational resource allocation decisions are generally most meaningful after students complete the ISCED 2 level of schooling. The IRR to ISCED 3 is therefore an indication of the value of staying in school to complete ISCED 3 after completing ISCED 2.

Four observations about these estimates of the returns to education are relevant:

- They are remarkably consistent among the different countries and with most of the estimates of the returns to education that have been previously published.
- They indicate that the increased earnings that result from increasing levels of education are, in almost every case, substantially greater than the costs that are incurred. In this regard, whenever possible, both public and private costs were included in the calculations, including estimates of foregone earnings. It should also be noted that these returns are expressed in real terms, *i.e. net* of inflation.
- The rate of return to women was below that of men in most cases (contrary to the results reported in other countries in the literature). This may be due, in part, to the fact that a greater percentage of women than men engage in part-time work in order to spend more time caring for children and managing a household. Unfortu-

nately, the state of the science does not enable us to incorporate these non-market benefits into our calculations.

• In four countries, the internal rates of return to men and women who completed ISCED 3 levels of education were greater than those to men and women who completed the ISCED 6/7 level.

In Annex 7.2, several limitations in the estimates of rates of return are discussed. Despite these limitations, the rates of return that were calculated appear to be reasonable, and an analysis of the results yields interesting and important observations, provided that the biases that exist in the data are taken into account.

### Sensitivity of Results to Assumptions about Missing or Limited Data

In the previous section, data from the INES database were used to estimate the social internal rate of return to upper secondary, non-university tertiary, and tertiary education in ten OECD countries (ISCED levels 3, 5, and 6/7. (It was possible also to calculate the rate of return for ISCED level 2 in three countries). In order to make these calculations, a number of assumptions had to be made which were applied uniformly across countries and educational levels. To the extent that these assumptions are less accurate for some countries than others, or for some levels of education than others, the calculated IRRs may lead to inappropriate inferences.

In order to test the sensitivity of the IRR indicator to several of these assumptions, additional calculations were carried out using a more detailed database that was available for the United States in order to determine whether an improved INES database would increase the accuracy of the rate of return calculations presented. It must, of course, be recognised that these results may not apply with equal force to other countries.

The sensitivity analysis clearly indicates that actual data on earnings for the age-groups below 25 have a very significant effect on estimates of foregone earnings and generally cause a reduction in the estimated IRRs, particularly for persons who complete ISCED levels 6/7. In the United States, this means that the measure of foregone earnings used in the OECD estimates understates the actual foregone earnings for students in tertiary education in the United States.

As expected, when the assumption is made that students have no earnings, the rate of return falls further yet. Although this assumption is not realistic for the United States, it may have applicability in some countries and could cause the estimates, as calculated for the OECD countries, to be significantly overstated. However, on the basis of US data, the bias will not be large.

### 4. Conclusions and Recommendations

The experimental calculations presented in the previous section are illustrative of what can be achieved with the calculation of an IRR indicator. However, missing data required several strong assumptions that limited the usefulness of these calculations. The estimates of the rates of return to different levels of education can be further improved by enhancing the quality of the data reported to the OECD.

The sensitivity analysis carried out on more extensive data about workers in the United States provides a strong basis for recommending that more detailed age break-downs be used. At a minimum, the following changes should be made:

- Information on earnings by educational attainment should be reported for workers over age 25 in at most 10-year age intervals. This only requires a small modification to the existing data structure for workers aged 25 and over. It would require that the 45 to 64-year age interval be split into 45 to 54 and 55 to 64 intervals.
- Information on earnings by educational attainment of workers below age 25 should be collected. This should be done in at least two age groupings: 16-19 and 20-24 years. Because earnings rise so quickly during the ages 16 to 24, it would be desirable to collect earnings data in even greater age detail. However, it is unlikely that the survey sample sizes used to collect these data would support the added detail.
- Information should be collected on the proportion of students who work, and on the average earnings of those who do. In some countries it is common for students to work part-time while enrolled in education at, for example, the ISCED 3 level (Germany) or ISCED 5 level (United States). The earnings from this employment may significantly reduce the cost and therefore increase the rate of return to these levels of education in these countries for these individuals.

Other areas of concern, but not leading to specific recommendations include:

- *The need for separate estimates of educational expenditures by ISCED level, particularly for ISCED 5 and 6/7:* the INES database currently aggregates all tertiary-level educational expenditures. However, expenditures per student can vary dramatically across different parts of tertiary education, which can then lead to changes in the internal rates of return to education at these levels. In the United States, for example, expenditure per pupil at ISCED 5 is on average one-third of that at ISCED 6/7. The inability to take account of differences in the costs of these different levels of education could misrepresent differences in the rate of return to these two types of education.
- *The need to include information on variation in the rate of return to education:* the internal rate of return calculated using the methodology outlined above applies best to individuals for whom the assumptions about the age of beginning and ending the additional education and the assumptions about work and earnings while a student are accurate. Changing these assumptions in line with the data for each country will illustrate the range of values which the internal rate of return can take for individuals following different paths through education, and can help policy-makers to decide whether to encourage or discourage certain paths. Three examples will clarify what is meant by paths and illustrate the value of report information on the variation in the rate of return to education:
  - In some countries, students can pursue education on a part-time basis, *i.e.* they can attend classes part-time and work part-time. These students will necessarily take longer to complete their education but will have lower foregone earnings.

If there are fixed costs associated with each enrolled student, whether he or she attends full or part-time, then public expenditures for the education of a given number of part-time students from first enrolment to completion may be higher than for the same number of full-time students.

- In most countries, in at least one ISCED level, there is considerable variation in the length of programmes or in the average earnings of graduates of different fields of study. Although data to support calculation of internal rates of return in different fields would be difficult to obtain, the results could be informative to policy-makers. For example, if students in some fields are likely to enjoy very high earnings, policy-makers may ask these students to pay for a greater proportion of their education than students in other fields that policy-makers regard as equally vital but for which the earnings benefits are smaller.

- In some countries, the age at which students begin their studies at the next ISCED level varies considerably. The reason could be that the student has been in the labour force working and has decided to return to education, or that the student has moved from a vocational education track to an academic education track, or that the student is repeating his or her studies at the same level but in a new field. The calculations above were based on the theoretical or typical ages of beginning and completing studies at each ISCED level. Calculating the IRR using a variety of beginning and completion ages, using each country's data, would illustrate the variability in the internal rate of return for different students in the country.

Education is one of many services that compete for public support. Information of the type provided by the Internal Rate of Return indicator can help policy-makers evaluate more accurately the benefits to public and private investment in education.

# Procedure of the Rate of Return Calculations

The internal rates of return to education reported in Table 7.2 required estimates of earnings at each age from the start of (non-compulsory) education to the age of retirement for those who complete each level of education. With these earnings data, data on educational costs, and a calculation formula readily available in spreadsheet software for personal computers, the internal rates of return can be easily calculated.

## Lifetime Earnings Estimates

The first step was to estimate the lifetime earnings of individuals in each country according to gender and ISCED level. For most of the countries, information was taken from the OECD INES database for Network B (Student Destinations) on earnings in 1992 of the population by age and ISCED level. Information was provided by gender and the following age-groups: 25 to 29, 30 to 34, 35 to 44, and 45 to 64. Estimates of earnings over a lifetime were developed from this cross-sectional information submitted by each country. The following operations were used:

 – First, it was assumed that persons only had earnings between the ages of 16 and 65.
 – Second, average earnings for each age range were applied to each age within the range. For example, the average earnings of workers aged 25 to 29 were used as the estimated earnings of persons aged 25, 26, 27, 28, and 29.
 – Third, to estimate the average earnings of persons aged 16 to 24, the average earnings of individuals aged 25 to 29 in that ISCED level were decreased by 10 per cent for each year of age between 16 and 24. Thus, the average earnings of persons aged 24 were assumed to be 90 per cent of the 25 to 29-year-old level, and persons aged 16 were assumed to have average earnings only 10 per cent of the 25 to 29-year-old age-group. These much lower earnings are plausible since young workers tend not only to work for lower wages, but also to work fewer hours during a year, particularly if attending school.
 – Fourth, longitudinal earnings were estimated from these cross-sectional data by assuming an annual rise in real earnings of one per cent per year. This is the rise in real earnings that would result from a relatively low growth rate in labour productivity. It was assumed that this percentage growth in earnings is the same for all countries and for all levels of education within countries.

## Increased Earnings after Education

The next step was to estimate the earnings benefit, $E_i$, of completing each higher level of education for each age, $i$, from completion of that level to age 65. The benefit is the difference between the average earnings of workers with successive levels of education. The average earnings of persons who completed ISCED 6/7 were compared to those who stopped at ISCED 3, not ISCED 5, because in most countries the choice of attending university or following another path is made at the end of ISCED 3. In only a few countries were there enough workers who stopped their education at ISCED 0/1 to make calculation of a difference between ISCED 2 and 0/1 feasible.

## Costs

The third step was to calculate the added costs of completing each higher level of education. Total education costs for each ISCED level are the sum of the direct costs, $C_i$, and foregone earnings $F_i$.

The direct costs, $C_i$, were estimated from data on average annual expenditure per pupil. Data contained in *Education at a Glance* (1993, Indicator P6) report the average annual expenditure per pupil on education for primary, secondary, and tertiary education in twelve OECD countries in 1991. It was assumed that these average annual expenditures were incurred for each year the student was enrolled at that ISCED level. In the case of secondary education, it was assumed that the average expenditure per year applied to both ISCED 2 and ISCED 3. In the case of tertiary education, the assumption was made that the average expenditure per year applied to both ISCED 5 and ISCED 6. These costs were applied at the ages at which a person would be expected to be enrolled in each ISCED level, which varied somewhat between countries. These estimated ages are reported in Table 7.3.

The foregone earnings, $F_i$, at age $i$ of students who continue to the next higher level of education are the average earnings of persons who did not continue, minus the average earnings of students at that level of education. To simplify the calculations, the earnings of students were

Table/Tableau 7.3.

**Typical ages for people enrolled in education at different levels of education**

*Âges typiques des élèves et étudiants à différents niveaux de formation*

| | ISCED level | | | |
|---|---|---|---|---|
| | Lower secondary education ISCED 2 | Upper secondary education ISCED 3 | Tertiary education, short duration ISCED 5 | Tertiary education, long duration ISCED 6/7 |
| Belgium | 13-16 | 17-19 | 20-22 | 20-24 |
| Denmark | 13-16 | 17-19 | 20-22 | 20-23 |
| Finland | 14-16 | 17-19 | 20-21 | 20-23 |
| France | 13-16 | 17-19 | 20-21 | 20-23 |
| Germany | 13-16 | 17-19 | 20-21 | 20-24 |
| Netherlands | 13-16 | 17-18 | 19-21 | 19-22 |
| Spain | 13-14 | 15-19 | – | 20-23 |
| Sweden | 13-15 | 16-18 | 19-20 | 19-22 |
| Switzerland | 13-16 | 17-19 | 20-21 | 20-26 |
| United States | 13-15 | 16-18 | 19-20 | 19-22 |

*Source:* Survey of Network B representatives.

estimated to be one-third of the earnings of non-students who did not continue to the next higher level of education. Therefore, foregone earnings of students at a particular ISCED level are simply two-thirds of the earnings of the non-students of the same age at the next lower ISCED level.

## Rate of Return Calculation

With these components, the rate of return to each ISCED level was calculated by finding the rate of discount, $r$, that would equate the present value of the costs of each ISCED level to the present value of increased earnings associated with completing that ISCED level. In symbols:

$$\frac{(C_{s-d} + F_{s-d})}{(1 + r)^{s-d}} + \ldots + \frac{(C_s + F_s)}{(1 + r)^s} = \frac{E_s + 1}{(1 + r)^{s+1}} + \ldots + \frac{E_{65}}{(1 + r)^{65}}$$

where $s$ is the age of completing the level of education and $d$ is the duration of that level of education.

Table 7.2 shows the internal rates of return that were calculated on the basis of information in the INES database for Network B and *Education at a Glance* (OECD, 1993) for ten countries for which there are both cost and earnings data.

This procedure estimates the private return to the social, *i.e.* private and taxpayer, cost of educating persons at the next higher ISCED levels. It is based on the creation of a lifetime earnings profile for men and women who attain different ISCED levels. Other researchers with access to more extensive data and with individual observations may use regression procedures (*e.g.* Gelderblom and de Koning, 1994) to account for other determinants of earnings. The procedure employed in this paper emphasises the perspective of the individual and ignores macro-economic effects that result when many individuals change their investment in education. At a macro-economic level, the rate of return to education depends on many additional factors including the state of technology, the size of the capital stock, the size of the labour force, and the differences in educational achievement among the population.

# Limitations of the Rate of Return Calculations

The estimates of rates of return have several limitations, which they share with most calculations of rates of return to education. These limitations should be kept in mind when interpreting the results.

Firstly, there are obvious problems of missing data and imprecision in the data that were provided by the OECD countries.

Secondly, the way in which costs were calculated for each ISCED level did not take account of differences in rates of return because some students at each ISCED level take longer than the standard amount of time to complete that level (Blaug, 1976).

Thirdly, there was no adjustment for differences in ability among persons who complete the same ISCED levels in different countries. One problem in making comparisons between countries is that the requirements for entering different levels of education vary, so that countries which tend to be more selective than others probably have persons of a higher ability in more advanced educational programmes. This problem may be partly offset if poverty or social class prevents some persons from achieving the educational levels that would be indicated by their ability.

Fourthly, there was no adjustment for differences in ability among persons who complete different ISCED levels. Persons who attain higher ISCED levels probably have more ability than those who do not, and part of the differences in earnings between the different levels is due to differences in abilities, rather the differences in educational attainments.

Fifthly, the comparison of ISCED levels does not take account of the fact that many workers receive extensive vocational training outside formal schooling through apprenticeship schemes and/or on-the-job training. This is a source of understatement of the returns to education since the comparison of higher and lower ISCED levels fails to take account of the full extent of the training that persons in lower ISCED levels may have achieved which has caused their earnings to rise. The returns to on-the-job training have been frequently discussed (*e.g.* Cohen, 1985; Miller, 1984; Psacharopoulos and Arriagada, 1986; Gelderblom and de Koning, 1994; Jimenez *et al.*, 1989; Mincer, 1962).

Sixthly, there was no adjustment for the likelihood that a worker will become unemployed, disabled, or suffer early death between the ages of 16 and 64. The size of the effects of these variables on rates of return is unclear. However, it is probably a greater source of understatement among persons in lower ISCED levels.

Finally, as previously noted, there are important benefits to education that are not included in these calculations.

# Sensitivity Analysis of Rates of Return

In order to determine whether more detailed information than is currently available in the INES database would improve the accuracy of the IRR calculations, further analyses were carried out using a more detailed database available for the United States. These data were used to determine how the use of actual and detailed data for the age-earnings distribution of non-students under age 25, and more detailed data for the age-earnings distribution of persons over age 45 would affect the rate of return calculations. In addition, different methods of estimating foregone earnings for students were examined.

## Earnings for Those Aged 24 and Below

No data on the earnings of people below the age of 25 are available in the INES database. The procedure, described in Annex 7.1, estimated earnings for each age between 16 and 25 by linearly interpolating between zero, the assumed earnings of 15-year-old and the average earnings of 25 to 29-year-olds.

To examine the effect of a more detailed earnings distribution for persons under age 25, IRRs were calculated using three differing procedures for estimating the earnings of persons under age 25. Each of these estimates used the same age-groups over age 24 as were available in the INES data and assumed that foregone earnings were equal to two-thirds of the earnings of persons in the next lowest ISCED level in the age range of the persons for whom an IRR was being calculated. The three IRRs involved the following differences in estimating earnings among persons below age 25:

- the earnings of non-students aged 16 to 24 in each ISCED level were interpolated exactly as was done when using the INES data;
- the actual earnings of non-students for each of the above years were used; and
- the earnings of students below age 25 were grouped into two age ranges, 16 to 19, and 20 to 24. This calculation was performed in order to utilise age ranges for which it would be realistic for the OECD to request data from Member countries.

The use of actual age-earnings information for persons under age 25 resulted in lower IRRs than the interpolation method used in calculating IRRs from the INES data, particularly for men who complete tertiary education (ISCED levels 6/7) and for women who complete non-university tertiary education (ISCED level 5; see Table 7.4). On the other hand, the IRRs did not change for men who complete upper secondary education (ISCED level 3). The IRR actually increased for women who complete upper secondary education when actual data on earnings were used.

**Rates of return to education in the United States using different methods of estimating earnings for persons under age 25, by gender and highest level of education attained, 1992**

*Taux de rendement de la formation aux États-Unis selon différentes méthodes de calcul des gains pour les personnes de moins de 25 ans, par sexe et niveau de formation maximal, 1992*

| Method of estimating earnings | Men | | | Women | | |
|---|---|---|---|---|---|---|
| | Upper secondary education ISCED 3 | Tertiary education, short duration ISCED 5 | Tertiary education, long duration ISCED 6/7 | Upper secondary education ISCED 3 | Tertiary education, short duration ISCED 5 | Tertiary education, long duration ISCED 6/7 |
| Interpolated | 18 | 10 | 13 | 16 | 10 | 13 |
| Single year, actual | 18 | 9 | 11 | 18 | 7 | 10 |
| Grouped years, 16-19, 20-24 | 18 | 9 | 10 | 18 | 7 | 10 |

For all practical purposes, the rate of return was not affected by the use of two age intervals under age 25 as compared to using each individual year of age.

An examination of US data on the earnings of workers under age 25 in the United States indicates that at least part of the reason for these results is that the earnings of individuals who complete tertiary education are overestimated in the age range 20 to 24, while the actual earnings of individuals who complete upper secondary education are very close to the interpolated estimates, as is seen in Table 7.5. Thus, the procedures used for the OECD countries overstate the IRR for persons who complete tertiary education.

### Ranges over Age 24

The INES data utilised four different age categories, *i.e.* 25-29, 30-34, 35-44, and 45-64 years. The procedure to calculate the IRR applied the average earnings in each age range to each individual in that age range. This could cause systematic overstatement or understatement of the earnings of individuals in specified ages. In particular, there was a concern about the broad age range 45 to 64 since imputing the same earnings to all persons in this age range would probably understate the actual average earnings of individuals in their forties, and overstate the average earnings of persons in their sixties.

To examine the effect of a more detailed earnings distribution for persons over age 25, IRRs were calculated using four different procedures. Each of these procedures utilised the interpolation method for estimating the earnings of persons under age 25, and each assumed that foregone earnings were equal to one-third of the earnings of persons in the next lowest ISCED level in the age range of the persons for whom an IRR was being calculated. They differed from the procedures used for the OECD estimates only in the way earnings data were grouped for the age ranges over age 24. These were grouped as follows:

- the same age ranges were employed as were used with the INES data;
- the age range over 45 was broken down into two age ranges, 45-54, and 55-64; and
- five-year age ranges were used between the ages of 25 and 64; and one-year age ranges were used between the ages of 25 and 64.

Table/Tableau 7.5.

**Actual earnings of persons with different highest levels of education attained compared to earnings estimated by interpolation method** (US$)

*Gains effectifs des personnes selon le niveau de la formation maximal par rapport aux gains estimés par interpolation*

| Age | Lower secondary education ISCED 2 | | Upper secondary education ISCED 3 | | Tertiary education, short duration ISCED 5 | | Tertiary education, long duration ISCED 6/7 | |
|---|---|---|---|---|---|---|---|---|
| | Actual | Estimate | Actual | Estimate | Actual | Estimate | Actual | Estimate |
| 16 | 4 771 | 1 357 | | | | | | |
| 17 | 4 365 | 2 715 | | | | | | |
| 18 | 7 404 | 4 072 | | | | | | |
| 19 | 7 066 | 5 430 | 8 540 | 7 856 | | | | |
| 20 | 8 754 | 6 787 | 10 049 | 9 820 | | | | |
| 21 | 9 215 | 8 145 | 12 824 | 11 784 | 12 920 | 13 306 | | |
| 22 | 10 399 | 9 502 | 13 350 | 13 748 | 12 648 | 15 524 | | |
| 23 | 10 134 | 10 860 | 14 264 | 15 712 | 15 776 | 17 742 | 15 728 | 21 744 |
| 24 | 13 050 | 12 217 | 15 797 | 17 676 | 17 604 | 19 960 | 20 363 | 24 462 |
| 25-29 | | 13 575 | | 19 640 | | 22 177 | | 27 180 |
| | Percentage error in estimate | | | | | | | |
| 16 | −72 | | | | | | | |
| 17 | −38 | | | | | | | |
| 18 | −45 | | | | | | | |
| 19 | −23 | | −8 | | | | | |
| 20 | −22 | | −2 | | | | | |
| 21 | −12 | | −8 | | 3 | | | |
| 22 | −9 | | 3 | | 23 | | | |
| 23 | 7 | | 10 | | 12 | | 38 | |
| 24 | −6 | | 12 | | 13 | | 20 | |

Table/Tableau 7.6.

**Rates of return to education in the United States by gender and highest level of education attained, 1992**

*Taux de rendement de la formation aux États-Unis par sexe et niveau de formation maximal, 1992*

| Age ranges over age 25 | Men | | | Women | | |
|---|---|---|---|---|---|---|
| | Upper secondary education ISCED 3 | Tertiary education, short duration ISCED 5 | Tertiary education, long duration ISCED 6/7 | Upper secondary education ISCED 3 | Tertiary education, short duration ISCED 5 | Tertiary education, long duration ISCED 6/7 |
| INES age ranges | 18 | 10 | 13 | 16 | 19 | 13 |
| INES ranges under age 45, 10 year ranges over age 45 | 18 | 10 | 13 | 16 | 11 | 13 |
| 5 year ranges, ages 25-64 | 18 | 10 | 13 | 16 | 10 | 13 |
| 1 year ranges, ages 25-64 | 18 | 10 | 12 | 16 | 10 | 13 |

There was almost no change for any groups defined by gender and ISCED level, as the different procedures were used to define the different age-earnings groups (see Table 7.6). In the case of persons aged 45 and over, this is probably because discounting causes earnings attributed to persons in their late 50s and 60s to contribute far less to the present value of earnings than earnings attributed to persons in their 40s and early 50s, even though their earnings are declining. To illustrate this phenomenon, the present value at age 25 of one unit of currency to be earned at age 55 is worth less than six per cent of the face value of that unit.

## Estimates of Foregone Earnings

As previously noted, no data on the earnings of students were reported to the OECD. Estimates of the internal rate of return may be particularly sensitive to these earnings. The less students work, the greater the level of foregone earnings, and the lower the rate of return to education. In the estimates for the OECD countries, students' earnings were assumed to be one-third of the level of the earnings of workers of the same age with the *next* lower level of education. In some countries, students frequently work during the summers and some have part-time jobs during the school year, although the amount of work varies considerably from country to country. To test the effect of different methods of estimating foregone earnings on the internal rate of return, internal rates of return in the United States were calculated using four procedures (see Table 7.7). Each of these procedures used the four age ranges for persons over age 24 that are reported to OECD. These procedures were:

Table/Tableau 7.7.

**Rates of return in the United States using different measures of foregone earnings, 1992**

*Taux de rendement de la formation aux États-Unis
selon différentes mesures du manque à gagner, 1992*

| Measures of foregone earnings | Men | | | Women | | |
|---|---|---|---|---|---|---|
| | Upper secondary education ISCED 3 | Tertiary education, short duration ISCED 5 | Tertiary education, long duration ISCED 6/7 | Upper secondary education ISCED 3 | Tertiary education, short duration ISCED 5 | Tertiary education, long duration ISCED 6/7 |
| Two-thirds of interpolated earnings | 18 | 10 | 13 | 16 | 10 | 13 |
| Two-thirds of actual earnings in age ranges 16-19 and 20-24 | 18 | 9 | 10 | 18 | 7 | 10 |
| Difference in actual earnings between students with earnings and non-students with earnings | 14 | 10 | 12 | 16 | 9 | 12 |
| Actual earnings of non-students | 12 | 9 | 11 | 13 | 8 | 10 |

1. The same method for interpolating earnings to persons below age 25 as was used for the OECD countries was employed; foregone earnings were estimated as two-thirds of interpolated earnings for the next lowest ISCED level;
2. Actual earnings in the age-groups 16 to 19 and 20 to 24 were used; foregone earnings were estimated as two-thirds of the actual earnings of persons in the next lowest ISCED level;
3. Actual earnings of students with earnings and non-students *with earnings* in each age-group were used; foregone earnings were estimated as the difference in these earnings levels; and
4. Actual earnings of non-students were used and students were assumed to have no earnings; foregone earnings were estimated to be the actual earnings of non-students with earnings.

The first two of the procedures used above were previously used when examining the effect of using actual earnings data for persons under age 25, and are presented as contrasting estimates for methods three and four.

Methods three and four were designed to provide upper and lower bounds to measures of foregone earnings. Method three utilises the difference between the average earnings of non-students and students with earnings to measure foregone earnings, and method four assumes that students have no earnings and that foregone earnings can be measured by the earnings of non-students in the next lowest ISCED level. Method three understates foregone earnings since a significant percentage of students do not work, and method four overstates foregone earnings since some students do work.

A comparison of methods one and two indicates that assuming students had one-third of the actual average earnings of persons in each age group resulted in a lower IRR (higher foregone earnings) for both men and women in tertiary education. It had no effect on the IRR of men who complete upper secondary education only, and actually increased the IRR of women in this educational category. As previously noted, this indicates that the earnings of persons who complete upper secondary education were higher than the estimates developed by the interpolation method for students in tertiary education.

An examination of methods three and four, which provide an upper and lower bound for estimates of foregone earnings, yielded two surprising conclusions:

- Firstly, the differences in IRRs between these two models were small, given that they were designed to represent upper and lower bounds to the effects of different measures of foregone earnings. The difference was usually about two percentage points, indicating that most alternative empirical measures of foregone earnings would not create major changes in the IRRs.
- Secondly, in most cases, the decrease in the IRR was relatively small when foregone earnings were assumed to be two-thirds of the actual earnings of the next lowest ISCED level (method two as compared to method one). The only exception was among men who completed ISCED 3. Apparently, the average earnings of persons who do not complete this level of education are considerably higher than those of their age counterparts who are still in school; the interpolated estimates used in this paper would assume that their earnings were only 10 to 20 per cent of the average among 25 to 29-year-old adults when they were 16 or 17. This low estimate of earnings may be realistic for all persons of that age, but is apparently too low in the case of students who have left school.

It is worth noting that since the ability levels of students presumably tend to be higher than the actual earnings of non-students of the same age, then foregone earnings may be higher than those calculated by methods three and four and the actual IRR lower than that indicated by these methods.

In sum, the procedure for estimating foregone earnings used for the OECD estimates (method one) appears to significantly underestimate the foregone earnings of upper secondary graduates, and probably has a smaller effect on the foregone earnings of the other gender/ISCED categories.

## Revised Estimate of IRR

The sensitivity analysis indicated that if OECD countries submitted somewhat more detailed information on earnings by ISCED level and age, then estimates of rates of return based on the INES database would be improved. The changes that are most feasible are:

- to obtain earnings information on persons under age 25 by two age categories, 16 to 19, and 20 to 24;
- to obtain earnings information on persons over age 45 by 10-year age categories; and
- to obtain information on earnings of students and non-students for ages below 25.

The effect of employing each of these changes in the US data are shown in Table 7.8. The first row shows the IRRs based on the procedures used for the OECD countries. The second row shows the IRRs obtained by: 1) using actual earnings data for persons under age 25; 2) using two age categories below age 25 and two above age 45; and 3) using actual earnings to estimate foregone earnings among students (method three above). The largest effect is on men who complete ISCED level 3, for whom the IRR fell by over 20 per cent. The other IRRs fell by only one percentage point (two cases), or not at all (three cases) as compared to the method developed for the OECD countries from INES data.

Table / Tableau 7.8.

### Rates of return in the United States, using different calculation procedures, 1992

*Taux de rendement de la formation aux États-Unis selon différents modes de calcul, 1992*

| Calculation procedures | Men | | | Women | | |
|---|---|---|---|---|---|---|
| | Upper secondary education ISCED 3 | Tertiary education, short duration ISCED 5 | Tertiary education, long duration ISCED 6/7 | Upper secondary education ISCED 3 | Tertiary education, short duration ISCED 5 | Tertiary education, long duration ISCED 6/7 |
| Procedures used with INES data | 18 | 10 | 13 | 16 | 10 | 13 |
| Procedures using more detailed data | 14 | 10 | 12 | 16 | 10 | 12 |

107

# References

ANGRIST, J.D. and KRUEGER, A.B. (1991), "Does compulsory school attendance affect schooling and earnings?", *The Quarterly Journal of Economics*, CVI, No. 4, pp. 979-1014.

BEHRMAN, J.R. and DEOLALIKAR, A.B. (1988), "Are there differential returns to schooling by gender?", *The Case of Indonesian Labour Markets*, unpublished manuscript.

BLAU, D.M., BEHRMAN, J.R., and WELFE, B.L. (1988), "Schooling and earnings distributions with endogenous labour force participation, marital status and family size", *Econometrica*, No. 55 (219), pp. 297-316.

BLAUG, M. (1976), "The rate of return on investment in education in Thailand", *Journal of Development Studies*, No. 12 (2), pp. 73-83.

BLAUG, M. (1979), "Economics of education in developing countries: current trends and new priorities", *Third World Quarterly*, No. 1 (1), pp. 73-83.

BLAUG, M. (1985), "Where are we now in the economics of education", *Economics of Education Review*, No. 4 (1), pp. 17-28.

CARD, D. and KRUEGER, A.B. (1992), "Does school quality matter? Returns to education and the characteristics of public schools in the United States", *Journal of Political Economy*, No. 100 (1), pp. 1-40.

COHEN, S.I. (1985), "A cost-benefit analysis of industrial training", *Economics of Education Review*, No. 4 (4), pp. 327-339.

GELDERBLOM, A. and DE KONING, J. (1994), "Learn how to earn – returns on educational careers: an analysis on the individual level", Paper for the Sixth EALE Conference, Warsaw, September, 1994, Netherlands Economic Institute, Department of Labour Market and Education, Rotterdam.

GRILICHES, Z. (1977), "Estimating the returns to schooling: some econometric problems", *Econometrica*, No. 45, pp. 1-22.

JALLADE, J.P. (1973), *The Financing of Education: An Examination of Basic Issues,* ERIC Document ED.

JIMENEZ, E., KUGLER, B., and HORN, R. (1989), *National In-service Training Systems in Latin America: An Economic Evaluation of Colombia's SENA*, World Bank Reprint Series No. 446, The World Bank, Washington, DC.

JORGENSON, D.W. and FRAUMENI, B.M. (1989), "Investment in education", *Educational Researcher,* Vol. 18 (4), pp. 35-44.

KHANDKER, S.R. (1989), *Returns to Schooling and Male-Female Differences in Peru*, The World Bank, Population and Human Resources Department, Washington, DC.

LESLIE, L.L. and BRINKMAN, P.T. (1993), *The Economic Value of Higher Education*, Oryx Press, Phoenix, AZ.

LEVIN, H.M. (1989), "Mapping the economics of education: an introductory essay", *Educational Researcher,* No. 18 (4), pp. 13-16.

LORENZ, W. and WAGNER, J. (1990), *A Note on Returns to Human Capital in the Eighties: Evidence from Twelve Countries,* The Luxembourg Income Study, Working Paper 54.

MCMAHON, W.W. and BOEDIONO. (1992), "Universal basic education: an overall strategy of investment priorities for economic growth", *Economics of Education Review*, No. 11 (2), pp. 137-151.

MILLER, P.W. (1984), "Education and the distribution of earned income", in R. Blandy and O. Covick (Eds.), *Understanding the Labour Markets*, Allen and Unwin, Winchester, MA.

MINCER, J. (1962), "On the job training: cost, returns, and implications", *Journal of Political Economy*, No. 70 (2), pp. 50-79.

MINCER, J. (1974), *Schooling, Experience and Earnings*, Columbia University Press, New York.

MINCER, J. (1989), "Human capital and the labour market: a review of current research", *Educational Researcher*, No. 18 (4), pp. 27-34.

OECD (1993), *Education at a Glance: OECD Indicators* (bilingual), 2nd edition, CERI, Paris.

PSACHAROPOULOS, G. (1992), "Evaluation of education and training: what room for the comparative approach?", Paper presented at the fifteenth annual conference of the Comparative Education Society in Europe, University of Bourgogne, Dijon, France.

PSACHAROPOULOS, G. (1993), *Returns to Investment in Education: A Global Update*, The World Bank, Washington, DC.

PSACHAROPOULOS, G. and ARRIAGADA, A.M. (1992), *The Educational Composition of the Labour Force: An International Update*, Background Paper No. 92/49, The World Bank, Washington, DC.

PSACHAROPOULOS, G. and WOODHALL, M. (1985), *Education for Development: An Analysis of Investment Choices*, Oxford University Press, New York.

SCHULTZ, T.P. (1988), "Education investments and returns", in H. Chenery and T. N. Srinivasan (Eds.), *Handbook of Development Economics*, North Holland Press, New York.

ST. JOHN, E. and MASTEN, C. (1990), "Returns to the federal investment in financial aid", *Journal of Student Financial Aid*, No. 20 (3), pp. 4-23.

WILLIS, R.J. and ROSEN, S. (1979), "Education and self-selection", *Journal of Political Economy*, No. 87 (5), Part 2.

WOODHALL, M. (1974), *The Investment Approach to Educational Planning: The Fundamentals of Educational Planning*, ERIC Document ED.

# Gender Disparities in Labour Market Outcomes of Education

## *Différences dans la situation des hommes et des femmes sur le marché du travail à l'issue de leur formation*

*by*

**Nicholas Pole**
Ministry of Education, Wellington, New Zealand

This chapter explores the range of indicators developed by Network B aimed at measuring the labour market outcomes for men and women resulting from their educational experiences. It highlights the background to the selection of a number of these indicators, and offers some explanation of key policy issues which are identified through the development of the indicator set and the results produced. Limitations in this work, particularly as it relates to the position of women in education and the labour market, are also highlighted, as are areas for further investigation. Gender has been a key bivariate employed in the collection of data for many of the indicators developed for the INES project, and in fact it is commonplace in standard labour market statistics. In this chapter, the composition of the labour market by educational attainment is integrated into a range of indicators. This allows an assessment to be made of the influence of the educational process on the labour market position of men and women.

*

\* \*

### Note de synthèse

*Ce chapitre examine les divers indicateurs élaborés par le Réseau B pour évaluer la situation des hommes et des femmes sur le marché du travail à l'issue de leur formation. Il explique pourquoi un certain nombre de ces indicateurs ont été retenus et analyse certaines questions de fond essentielles que la construction de ces indicateurs a mises en lumière ainsi que les résultats obtenus.*

*Il est courant que, dans les statistiques du marché du travail, les données soient ventilées par sexe. Cette ventilation est également utilisée dans les données recueillies pour le projet INES. Les indicateurs des effectifs, de la scolarisation et des flux d'élèves et les indicateurs des résultats des systèmes ont révélé certaines disparités entre la situation des hommes et celle des femmes ainsi que des différences sensibles entre pays. Nulle part les divers indicateurs mis au point ne donnent les mêmes résultats pour les hommes et les femmes, ce qui montre bien combien il importe d'élaborer des mesures spécifiques des différences selon le sexe dans le domaine de l'enseignement.*

*Dans ce chapitre, la composition de la population active selon le niveau de formation est intégrée dans plusieurs indicateurs. On peut aussi évaluer l'influence de l'enseignement sur la situation des hommes et des femmes au regard du marché du travail. Bien que les résultats ne reflètent pas toute la complexité des facteurs sociaux, culturels et économiques qui contribuent à différencier la situation des hommes et des femmes dans la société et l'activité économique, ils permettent cependant de juger du rôle que joue l'enseignement dans certains des résultats observés.*

*Enfin, l'auteur montre les limites de ce type de recherche, en particulier lorsqu'il s'agit de la situation des femmes dans l'enseignement et sur le marché du travail. Il mentionne en outre plusieurs domaines qui appellent des recherches plus poussées.*

\*

\*    \*

## 1. The Context for Labour Market Analysis of Gender Disparities

Throughout the work of INES, a range of differences between men's and women's positions, and considerable inter-country differences, have been identified through indicators on participation in education, flows through education, and system outcomes. In no country have similar results for males and females been found across the range of education indicators developed through the work of the Technical Group or in the networks. This reinforces the perception of very different educational experiences by men and women throughout the OECD. On many of the indicators developed for this project, women appear somewhat advantaged relative to men. This is especially highlighted by the two student graduation indicators R5 and R6 which are included in the third edition of *Education at a Glance* (OECD, 1995). At the upper secondary level, more women than men graduate (R11). Particularly marked is the advantage which exists for women in Denmark, Finland, Ireland and Portugal. In only five of the OECD countries which participated in this indicator were there greater proportions of men graduating. This may be a result of the apprenticeship training programmes which exist in these countries, and the disproportionate numbers of men who enrol in such programmes. Although the differential is less pronounced than at ISCED 3, and there is greater diversity between countries, there is a slight advantage for women in tertiary education also, where slightly higher graduation rates are recorded by women at first-degree level (R12). At significant variance with this trend is the low proportion of women graduates relative to men in Japan, Switzerland and Turkey, while women significantly outperform men in Canada, Denmark, Norway, Spain (in the *Diplomado*), Sweden, and the United States.

The higher rates of graduation by women in many OECD countries at both ISCED 3 and ISCED 6 levels could be thought to lead to greater opportunities for women, but as the analysis and description of the Network B indicators will show, this is not true. In part, the level of inequality for women within the labour market relative to their apparently more equitable position in the education system might reflect recent changes in education. The implementation of a range of educational policies and practices by a number of OECD countries in the 1980s, which were specifically oriented at removing many of the inequalities between men and women in education (OECD, 1993*a*), has had some impact on the distribution of opportunities. These changes in themselves reflect and have been accompanied by significant changes in attitudes towards the role of women in society and in economic life. But the gains by women in education in recent decades may be too new to have had a substantial effect on the labour market. By using an age cohort approach, many of the indicators of labour market outcomes developed as part of the INES project help to plot not only changes in the relative position between men and women over time but also the influence of education on this process. Key indicators in this respect are those that assess the educational attainment of the population and rates of labour force participation by men and women (C1, C2 and C11). Although the indicators developed by the Technical Group and other INES networks do provide some time series data, their origin is too recent to identify what may be large changes in the education of women relative to men and the resulting outcomes in the labour market.

It may also be true that, while in some respects educational equity between the sexes has been achieved, women and men continue to be channelled into very different career paths through subject selection and opportunities provided during their school careers. This is highlighted by those indicators that show graduation by fields of study (R14 and R15 in *Education at a Glance,* OECD, 1995). The high proportion of science and engineering degrees awarded to men is not matched by women. Women are found to be significantly under-represented in natural science, mathematics and computer sciences, with only a few countries achieving similar proportions of male and female graduates in these fields. Engineering is still almost entirely a pursuit of men throughout all OECD countries.

The different concentration of men and women in tertiary programmes results in part from the very different paths of study pursued by men and women in upper secondary education. The different exposure of males and females to various curricula may come from structural boundaries and guidance or through the more subtle effects of choice combined with social expectations. The impact of this exposure to particular areas of the curriculum can be investigated in the labour market by assessing the level of existing occupational and industrial segregation. This is an area where Network B has focused some attention since the collection of data for the second edition of *Education at a Glance* (OECD, 1993*b*).

## 2. Gender as a Unit of Analysis in the INES Project

Whereas many of the indicators developed for the INES project have captured data by gender, indicators aimed specifically at assessing gender differences in education have tended to be overlooked. While participation differentials provide one measure of gender equity within particular countries, they do not provide an adequate measure of the different experiences of girls and boys in education. For example, the lower number of women among science and engineering graduates is likely to reflect the very different subject selection paths taken by boys and girls throughout their school careers. Clearly, indicators of the exposure of girls and boys to various subject domains at various levels would help in assessing the factors which lead to this outcome. In addition, the concentration on male-dominated domains (as in the case of science and engineering graduates included in the indicator R15), might be at the cost of providing details on the fields in which the other 90 per cent of women graduates in OECD countries are concentrated.

As they focus on economic activity, these indicators cannot assess the contributions of men and women to activity outside the formal economy – for example, their contribution in the informal sector and towards the care and nurturing of children and other family members. Yet an awareness of these contexts, including changes in family formation patterns, the roles adopted by men and women outside the formal economy and the level of support provided by the state and other agencies and institutions, can have a substantial influence on describing men's and women's involvement with the labour force.

The availability of international indicator sets developed through the INES project allows for three key approaches towards the analysis of gender. Firstly, comparisons of differentials between men and women for individual countries may be made in order to assess the relative level of equality between the sexes among OECD countries. Secondly, the position of either men or women can be independently compared across countries in order to assess their relative labour market position. Thirdly, the gains made by men and women resulting from education may be compared over generations to assess the mechanisms which have contributed to change. An area of analysis not yet undertaken within the INES project is the investigation of the inter-relationship between the indicators developed within and across population groups.

## 3. ISCED and the Analysis of Gender

The utility and limitations of the ISCED system in developing cross-national indicators of education have been discussed in Chapters 2 and 3. There is, however, an important adjunct to this discussion if comparisons by gender are to be considered.

The classification of programmes according to ISCED can in itself reflect the traditional bias given to the qualifications generally pursued by men and women, since in some cases qualifications in domains which have traditionally been dominated by women are classified at lower levels of ISCED than those qualification areas that have been more general or the domain of men.

The aggregation of both general and vocational qualifications at ISCED 3, which has been adopted in the work on indicators, largely because of data classification problems and sample constraints in many countries, also tends to hide what may be significant variations in education policy and practices at this level. The concentration of men or women in one or the other form of education at ISCED 3 within a country may lead to significant differences in labour market outcomes. As an example, whereas women may hold general qualifications at this level, qualifications held by males may be more likely to be in trade and vocational fields, which return a higher premium in the labour market.


## 4.  Gender Differences in Educational Attainment

The combined effects of men's and women's different educational experiences over a number of decades can be identified by examining the proportion of men and women holding qualifications at various educational levels in the population. Education has a marked effect on labour market opportunities and outcomes. Skill levels influence participation in the labour market, occupational mobility and (of particular concern for women) the ability to move in and out of the labour force. Education can also work to reduce the risk of unemployment and underemployment. The different qualifications pursued by men and women, and the fields in which these qualifications are obtained, can also contribute towards segregation in the labour force since different skill acquisition results in the channelling of the sexes into very different career paths, in which promotional opportunities and monetary rewards may vary substantially. Access to adult education and training may also be more limited, further maintaining inequity.

Analysis of the educational attainment of the population by age gives some indication of the level of change which has taken place over time. Big differences in educational attainment between generations may mean that some countries have expanded their education systems, and increased the level of access and equality in education for population groups previously less advantaged.

One distorting effect in such analysis is international migration, which can alter the overall educational profile of the population. This is particularly true if migrants are selected for particular skills. This may also lead to gender differences within the overall educational profiles of the population, as in the case of those recruited for heavy manual occupations or for the service sector. The classification of overseas qualifications can in some cases also prove problematic for statisticians, resulting in migrants' being inconsistently assigned education codes. Thus far, Network B has not attempted to investigate the influence of international migration on the labour market.

Educational attainment indicators developed through Network B (C2) show substantial differences between men and women in levels of education (see Chapter 9). In the population aged 25-64 years, women are generally over-represented among those with lower secondary or primary qualifications and under-represented among those with university qualifications. Only in Ireland, Sweden and Turkey are there higher proportions of men with qualifications at lower secondary level and below (ISCED 0/1/2). By comparison, in no country did higher proportions of women hold university qualifications. Among non-university tertiary qualifications (ISCED 5) there are, however, marked variations between countries in the representation of women. While women are more likely than men to hold qualifications at this level overall, in Finland, Germany, Norway, Sweden and Switzerland, men are significantly over-represented among those holding such qualifications. This probably reflects the higher concentration of tertiary-level trade, craft and technician training in these countries and the predominance of men, who have generally pursued such qualifications. In comparison, in Australia, Belgium, France, New Zealand, Portugal and the United Kingdom, women predominate among those gaining non-university tertiary qualifications. As mentioned earlier, this reflects the types of education programme taught at this level.

## 5.  An Index of Gender Differences in Education

In order to provide a measure of the overall difference within a country in the educational profile of men and women, Network B has explored two potential indicators: an index of dissimilarity and an advantage index (for a technical discussion of the methods, see Chapter 9).

### The Dissimilarity Index

The index of dissimilarity provides a measure of the accumulated inequality between men and women in the population in terms of educational attainment. It is a measure of the percentage of women who would need to change their qualifications in order to gain the same qualifications profile as men. Having a single index for each country enables inter-country comparisons of men's and women's educational attainment to be made. This also allows for within-country comparisons between age cohorts. Such comparisons – say between the population aged 25-34 years and an older cohort or the total population – provide an assessment of the relative change in the level of educational equality between the sexes over time and indicate changes in the access, participation and outcomes for women in education relative to men. Results for this indicator, published in *Education at a Glance* (OECD, 1993), show that the degree of variance in educational attainment by gender was largest in Australia, Austria, New Zealand and Switzerland. In these countries, between 18 per cent and 24 per cent of women would have to obtain a qualification at a different level in order to achieve parity with men. In Germany, the Netherlands, and the United Kingdom a change of between 10 per cent and 15 per cent would be required. Countries with relatively small differences in the educational profile of men and women included Belgium, Canada, Finland, Italy, Norway, Portugal and Sweden. In these countries, less than five per cent of women would be required to change their educational qualifications in order to gain parity with men.

The very low value recorded for Portugal results from the high concentration of this population (93 per cent) at ISCED 0/1/2. This is also the case in Spain, where only 22 per cent of the population have a qualification at a level higher than ISCED 2.

Comparisons for the total population with those aged 25-34 years indicate some significant changes in the relative educational attainment of men and women. France, Germany, the Netherlands, the United Kingdom and the Czech and Slovak Republics each record marked reductions in the index of dissimilarity calculated for those aged 25-34 years, compared with that for the populations aged 25-64 years. This is indicative of considerable moves towards equality in educational attainment in these countries over recent decades. More moderate changes for this age-group were recorded in Austria and the United States. The distributions for Ireland, Portugal, Sweden and Turkey were more dissimilar at ages 25-34 than they are for the population as a whole, though the differences were small.

In the case of Sweden, this change comes about through bigger reductions in the proportion of women at ISCED 0/1/2, while in Ireland many more women have upper secondary qualifications relative to men. In Turkey, the advantage has shifted towards men among those aged 24-34 years who have completed upper secondary qualifications.

## The Advantage Index

While the index of dissimilarity provides a measure of variation, it does not provide information on how much anyone may be advantaged or disadvantaged as a result, simply because the focus is on comparing the distribution of the sexes at each level. In developing the Network B project, a further indicator, the advantage index, has been investigated in order to add greater weight to the results provided through the index of dissimilarity. This indicator, derived from the same data source, is able to show whether the overall differentials identified above are in favour of men or women. It is based on the difference in educational attainment for men and women at ISCED 0/1/2, less the difference at ISCED 5-7. It assumes that if the variation between men and women is greater among higher qualifications, then the group achieving the higher score is more advantaged than the other group (see Chapter 9). Clearly, those with a tertiary qualification have much greater marketability than those with no qualifications or only a lower secondary qualification.

In Australia, where the largest dissimilarity between men and women is identified, women have the advantage over men in higher educational qualifications, primarily as a result of their concentration in ISCED 5. At the other extreme, German and Swiss men have a significant advantage over women in higher qualifications. For nearly all other OECD countries, the advantage remains in favour of men.

While on the surface the low figure for Sweden suggests considerable equity between men and women in that country, this result disguises a substantial difference among men and women with non-university tertiary qualifications, women being more likely to have ISCED 5 qualifications and men ISCED 6.

A drawback with this indicator is that it provides no estimate of the influence of variations in the measure of dissimilarity at ISCED 3, but it is in attainment at this level where some of the largest variances between men and women may be identified.

Men significantly outnumber women in Australia, Austria, New Zealand, and the United Kingdom in attainment at ISCED 3 level. In these countries, such qualifications are likely to be predominantly among trades and crafts, which are typically a preserve of men. Although the differentials are somewhat lower, women are over-represented at this level in Canada, Switzerland and the United States. In these countries, this may reflect the lower proportion of women pursuing further qualifications of any kind following high school graduation.

While not attempted here, a further refinement to the advantage index could be made by providing weights for educational attainment based on the length of time required to obtain a qualification at a particular level. Such an indicator would then facilitate comparisons between the accumulated length of time men and women in different age cohorts and countries spend in education, and the advantage this brings in the labour market.

## 6. Educational Attainment and Labour Market Participation

As well as being influenced by economic, political and welfare conditions, the level of women's participation in the labour force itself influences overall levels of labour force participation within a country. Between-country variation in female labour force participation in fact accounts for much of the variation identified when a population's economic activity is compared. Labour force participation by women is explainable in terms of educational level as well as in terms of social and cultural values. Education can work to alter substantially a range of social and labour market outcomes, and it invariably leads to the questioning of traditional roles and norms. Education beyond the post-compulsory age can result in later childbearing, and it will generally lead women into a career, entailing further delays in childbearing, smaller family size, and less time out of the labour force after childbearing. Higher levels of education may also reduce the risk of unemployment and assist in the return to employment following a break, a feature particularly important for women, who often leave the labour force for childbearing. Educational attainment at the upper secondary level and beyond may also make the pursuit of further education and training, and of upgrading skills and qualifications, considerably easier than is the case for those with more limited education.

Throughout the OECD, levels of female labour force participation vary markedly, and in no country is female labour force participation above that of men, although overall levels of labour force participation recorded by Swedish women are higher than those achieved by men in a number of other OECD countries.

Female labour force participation is well below the average for the OECD in Ireland, Italy, Spain and Turkey; very high rates of participation are recorded by women in Denmark, Finland and Norway, as well as in Sweden. The rates of economic activity by women are rising at an average annual rate of two per cent over the past decade in the OECD countries (Core, 1994). This is a rate twice that of men, whose numbers in the labour force are decreasing in the majority of countries. The reduction in men's participation in the labour force has come about as a result of the two-fold influence of higher enrolments and retention in education, and of larger numbers of older men withdrawing from the labour force through retirement schemes and disability pensions (OECD, 1994).

Table 8.1 shows that for both men and women, labour force participation is highly correlated with educational attainment. Women attaining no higher than primary-level education are half as likely to be in the labour force as women with a university award. While this same trend is true for men, the difference between the participation of men at ISCED 0/1 and that of men at ISCED 6/7 is much smaller. The narrowing of the gap between men's and women's labour force participation, as women's educational attainment increases, supports the conclusion that education is a considerable force for change in the lives of women.

While this general pattern of improvement is repeated by younger women, the advantage from education is generally lower, with higher labour force participation also being recorded by those women with lower qualifications. A notable exception is Turkey, where there is little difference in the level of participation in the labour force by women aged 25-34 with ISCED 0/1 qualifications in comparison to the participation rates for women aged 25-64, whereas at ISCED 6/7 there is a marked improvement. In the latter case, the participation is at a level equivalent to that recorded for the OECD as a whole, and at higher levels than for women in half of the OECD countries. Turkish women aged 25-34 with a university qualification are three times as likely to be in the labour force as those women with only primary or lower qualifications. It should be remembered, however, that very few women in Turkey have qualifications at this level, and two-thirds of women in Turkey do not participate in the formal labour force. The influence of educational attainment on participation by young women was found to be most marked in Belgium, Ireland, Italy, the Netherlands and Spain, in addition to Turkey (see OECD, 1995).

Table/Tableau 8.1.

**Average rate of labour force participation for men and women in OECD countries by level of education attained (25-64 years of age), 1991**

*Taux moyen d'activité masculine et féminine dans les pays de l'OCDE par niveau de formation (25-64 ans), 1991*

| ISCED level | Number of countries | Men (%) | Women (%) | Difference (%) |
|---|---|---|---|---|
| Early childhood and primary education | 12 | 74.1 | 35.7 | 38.4 |
| Lower secondary education | 20 | 85.3 | 54.2 | 31.1 |
| Upper secondary education | 20 | 90.6 | 69.3 | 21.3 |
| Tertiary education, short duration | 16 | 93.1 | 80.6 | 12.5 |
| Tertiary education, long duration | 20 | 94 | 84.2 | 9.8 |

*Source:* OECD (1993b).

119

## 7. Labour Market Segregation

Higher participation in the labour force may not in itself be representative of increasing equality between the sexes. Rates of participation say nothing about the quality of employment. While this may be assessed to a degree by measuring income, income measures are not always directly comparable, particularly as women may be more highly concentrated in part-time as opposed to full-time employment. Quality of employment can also be measured through employment conditions, set either through national or regional legislation or through negotiated contracts with employers. Women's overall levels of labour force participation may be influenced by a range of employment conditions which recognise the reproductive role of women and their substantial commitment to work outside the paid labour force: for example, the ability to work part-time, parental leave, job security, provision of child care (and the kind of child care). The identification of these factors adds an important contextual element to the analysis of the indicators, as they result in a complex set of positive and negative outcomes. Part-time work, for example, may result in considerable inequities if women are limited to part-time work because of a lack of alternatives, and if workers are eligible for few of the benefits (sick leave, holidays or superannuation) which exist for full-time employees. The increase in the proportion of women pursuing part-time work may also have the effect of lowering wages for such work and lead to further casualisation. The incidence and level of part-time work has not been pursued by Network B, although it could be a rewarding area for investigation.

Throughout the OECD, women tend to be concentrated in a narrow range of industries, with many in the service sector (Core, 1994). Given this concentration, changes in the labour market are likely to affect men and women in very different ways. Indicators on the occupational and industrial distribution of the employed population by educational attainment allow an assessment of the level of segregation across countries as well as of the skill composition of these industries and occupational groups within countries. Through identification of skill levels, some of the vulnerability to changes in the labour market can be assessed. Higher concentrations of women in unskilled service sector jobs, for example, is believed to have resulted in these women being hardest hit by such changes (Core, 1994). However, even when women are found to be more than equally represented in terms of a particular occupational group, it is generally found that men have higher promotion prospects and ultimately greater seniority.

## 8. Gender Differences in Unemployment

The lower levels of labour force participation experienced by less qualified men and women may also be associated with non-availability of employment and the groups' marginalised labour market position. The evidence above suggests that women without qualifications are in a worse position than men in this respect, although further analysis is required to test the truth of this proposition.

Consistent definitions of unemployment throughout the OECD are difficult. In the data collected for the 1991 indicators published in *Education at a Glance* (OECD, 1993), unemployment was found to be highest in Ireland and Spain, with rates running at over twice the average for the OECD. Since 1991, while the relative position of most OECD countries has been sustained, the level of unemployment throughout the OECD has witnessed some significant changes. Across the OECD, women on average experience higher levels of unemployment than men, although there are large variations from country to country. The mean for the OECD is influenced considerably by Belgium, Italy and Spain, where unemployment among women is more than double that recorded by men. In Spain, female unemployment was almost three times that of men, the rates for Spanish women being significantly higher than those for men or women in any other OECD country.

While the overall rates of unemployment for young men and women aged 15 to 24 years are considerably closer, rates at this level are substantially higher than they are for the population as a whole. More than two-thirds of young women in the labour force in Italy and Spain were unemployed in 1991. The rates for men in these countries were high but still significantly lower than those of the women. In Australia, Italy and New Zealand, unemployment among young women was, however, significantly below that of young men. The considerably higher levels of unemployment at these younger ages, particularly for those with few skills, highlights the importance of developing indicators which plot the transition of young men and women between school and working life. It would be particularly important to identify those factors which appear to provide an advantage to men (or in a limited number of countries, an advantage to young women). In Australia and New Zealand, education provides one key to this process as young women remain in school longer, leave with higher qualifications, and transfer into post-secondary education and training programmes in higher numbers than young men. The processes contributing to this are complex and may in some cases be due to an initial lack of alternatives for young women within the labour market.

Given the low levels of labour force participation for women in some countries, the measurement of unemployment can prove to be a problem, as it may hide or disguise "true" levels of unemployment. Where attempts to gain employment have proved fruitless, women may be more likely to withdraw, or to be excluded, from the labour force. Among the OECD countries, women form the majority of discouraged workers, particularly in France, the Netherlands and Portugal, although the proportion of men has been increasing (OECD, 1994). This phenomenon will vary markedly from country to country and will be dependent on social and cultural contexts as well as government welfare and labour market policy, particularly as these contexts relate to the rights of women, the recognition of the labour market status of married women, and the mixture of welfare policies and support for married women and women in lone parent situations.

## 9. Education and Earnings

Possibly the most crucial indicators for examining the position of men and women in the labour market are those which assess the relative earnings from work (R22). The concentration of women in a narrow range of occupations, their different pay rates from men for similar work, their broken career paths and loss of tenure caused by leaving the labour force for childbearing, the higher concentration of women in part-time work, the less frequent promotion of women to senior positions, and the lower status given to traditional female occupations, are all seen as leading to the earnings gap between men and women (Hyman, 1981). These processes are moulded by social attitudes related to the role of women in the economy and within the workplace. Education has long been seen as a key to higher earnings and better labour market prospects (Cohen and Geske, 1990). The lower overall educational attainment of women has thus been seen as a factor in leading to women's overall lower incomes. Analysis of the returns from education has, however, generally concentrated on the population as a whole, with little consideration of the differential experience of men and women. As has already been shown in this chapter, education has a marked influence on individual participation in the labour market, particularly in the case of women. Education can also substantially reduce the risk of unemployment.

Results here show that in all countries studied, women earn substantially lower incomes from their labour market activity than men. Looking at relative earnings from work, however, reinforces the general theory that the average annual earnings from work increase with educational attainment. This study has also shown that the returns from education improve with age as the earnings gaps between ISCED levels become wider (see also Chapter 7).

For women, the returns from education are generally greater than those for men. Women in Australia with a university qualification, for example, can expect to earn 75 per cent more than those with only an upper secondary qualification and almost 95 per cent more than those with only primary or lower qualification, whereas Australian men with a university qualification receive less than 60 per cent more than men with an upper secondary qualification. A similar situation is noticeable in Canada, the Netherlands and Switzerland, and may indicate that in these countries women are doubly disadvantaged, both by their gender, and by lack of work skills and qualifications.


## 10. Conclusion


This chapter has identified the importance of the range of indicators developed through the INES project in providing a measure of the relative position of men and women in the labour force and the educational factors which in some way have led to this situation. While this indicator set does not uncover the complex web of social, cultural and economic factors which contribute to the differential position of men and women in society and in economic activity, it offers insights into the role that education has played in leading to some of the outcomes identified here and provides a pointer to further investigation and research. Education is clearly a key change mechanism in the lives of both men and women. It can also help a nation to achieve greater economic strength and productivity through harnessing and rewarding the talents of all its citizens.

# References

COHEN, E. and GESKE, T.G. (1990), *The Economics of Education,* 3rd edition, Pergamon Press, Oxford.

CORE, F. (1994), ''Women and the restructuring of employment'', *OECD Observer*, OECD, Paris, p. 186.

HYMAN, P. (1981), ''Women and pay'', *New Zealand Journal of Industrial Relations,* No. 6, pp. 79-89.

HYMAN, P. (1993), ''The earnings gap and pay equity. Developments in five countries'', in P. Morrison (Ed.), *Labour, Employment and Work in New Zealand*, Victoria University of Wellington, Wellington, New Zealand.

NORDIN, A. (n.d.), ''The gap between women's and men's earnings'', unpublished manuscript, Statistics Sweden, Stockholm.

OECD (1993*a*), ''Working party on the role of women in the economy'', unpublished discussion note, Paris.

OECD (1993*b*), *Education at a Glance: OECD Indicators* (bilingual), 2nd edition, CERI, Paris.

OECD (1994), *The OECD Jobs Study: Evidence and Explanations*, Paris.

OECD (1995), *Education at a Glance: OECD Indicators*, 3rd edition, CERI, Paris.

# Methodological Issues in the Calculation of an Index of Gender Differences

## *Problèmes méthodologiques posés par le calcul d'un indice des disparités entre les hommes et les femmes*

*by*

**Luc Van de Poele**
University of Ghent,
for the Ministry of the Flemish Community, Department of Education, Belgium

This chapter offers an overview of the techniques for calculating an index of gender differences in educational attainment that have been considered in Network B: ratio values, the dissimilarity index, the newly developed advantage index, and the index of years of schooling. None of these indices meets all the criteria of quality that are advanced in this chapter, *e.g.* general attainment invariance, directionality, and a concrete meaning. For some indicators, adjustment methods are presented which may overcome some of the drawbacks identified.

\*

\*      \*

## Note de synthèse

*Ce chapitre présente une vue d'ensemble des techniques utilisées pour calculer les quatre indices de niveaux de formation par sexe qui ont été examinés par le Réseau B. Ces quatre indices sont les suivants : i) ratios; ii) indice de disparité; iii) indice d'avantage; et iv) indice de durée de la scolarité.*

*Pour faciliter l'analyse des différents concepts, méthodes de calcul et modes de présentation graphique employés dans les trois éditions de* Regards sur l'éducation

(OCDE, 1992, 1993 et 1995), *on a introduit une série de critères qui définissent les caractéristiques souhaitables des indicateurs du niveau de formation par sexe. Le principal critère est l'invariance du niveau général de formation : autrement dit, un indice doit mesurer les disparités entre les hommes et les femmes, quel que soit le niveau général de formation de la population du pays. Autres critères importants : l'évolution, l'invariance en fonction de l'organisation et de la taille de la population, la normalisation rationnelle et l'interprétabilité.*

*La conclusion de cette analyse est que les ratios et l'indice de disparité ne répondent pas aux critères précités. Pour combler certaines de ces lacunes, le Réseau B a mis au point un nouvel indicateur : l'indice d'avantage. Cet indice repose sur l'hypothèse que le fait d'avoir suivi un cycle complet d'études supérieures confère un avantage sur le marché du travail et que les personnes qui n'ont pas achevé leurs études secondaires de deuxième cycle sont défavorisées. L'auteur montre aussi comment on peut calculer un indice d'avantage pour les pays Membres de l'OCDE en se fondant sur les données recueillies par le Réseau B. Il constate que l'indice d'avantage n'est pas facile à interpréter, mais donne un complément d'information sur l'évolution.*

\*

\*    \*

## 1. Introduction

Network B has developed new indicators on the contexts and outcomes of education. The network has also examined new data sources, created new calculation formulas, and explored new ways of presenting the information. A good example of this on-going search for improved indicators is the issue of gender differences. In the first three editions of *Education at a Glance* (OECD, 1992, 1993, 1995), data were presented showing the differences in educational attainment between men and women. But each version used different formulas, different methods of graphical presentation, and different concepts. This chapter explores how the discussion evolved. Four major techniques have been considered in the network, of which the first three have actually been published: ratio values, the dissimilarity index, the newly developed advantage index; and the index of years of schooling. For the purpose of this overview, a set of criteria is introduced that identifies desirable characteristics of measures of gender inequality. Each of the four indices is tested in the light of these criteria. For some of the indices, this chapter also presents adjustments that overcome some of the identified drawbacks. Many examples are given of the way in which the indices are calculated in practice. All tested measures use the same data source, namely the network's database stored at Statistics Sweden in Örebro, which chiefly contains data derived from labour force surveys but also uses census and administrative data.

## 2. Criteria for Measures of Gender Differences in Educational Attainment

- *General attainment invariance*: an index of gender differences should only measure the differences between men and women, irrespective of the general attainment level of a country's population. Gender differences in the lower ISCED categories should have the same weight as gender differences in the higher categories (*cf.* definitions in Chapter 3: Annex 3.1).
- *Directionality*: gender differences in educational attainment favour men or women. Indicators relating educational attainment to income or (un)employment confirm that high levels of educational attainment confer advantages (Fossett and South, 1983). An index of gender differences should therefore indicate in what direction the advantage operates. The Network B data permit comparisons of educational attainment between age-groups such as 25 to 34-year-old and 55 to 64-year-old. These comparisons show a certain degree of development over time. The index should incorporate such developments and give valid and clear information about the evolution of directionality in gender differences.
- *Concrete meaning*: the index should be easy to interpret and have concrete meaning in terms of the number of people with a certain level of education. The design of the index must be comprehensible to the average reader (Merschrod, 1981).
- *Organisational invariance* means that the index is not affected either by the combination of two units (ISCED categories) which have an identical pattern of segregation, or by the division of single categories into units with identical segregation patterns (Watts, 1992). Since not all countries deliver data for all ISCED categories, an index is preferred that is unaffected by the way in which data are aggregated.
- *Size invariance* refers to the invariance of the index if the population is increased proportionately. The gender differences in a country must not depend on the size of its population. If they do, it is impossible to compare different countries correctly. The aim is to measure the difference in educational attainment of men and women in different countries. This result must not be biased by different sizes of the population.
- *Rational normalisation*. If a concentration measure has the value 1 for perfect concentration and 0 for perfect dispersion, the value of 0.5 should represent 50 per cent concentration (Bonckaert and Egghe, 1991).

## 3. Ratio Values

In the first edition of *Education at a Glance* (OECD, 1992), the gender differences were presented as a sex ratio: the number of women per 100 men in each ISCED category. The network also discussed the possibility of choosing a ratio of men to every 100 women, since the female population is the basis of comparison.

Not the percentage, but the number of people in an ISCED category, was used to determine the ratio. Depending on the total number of men and women in the age-group, the ratio of the totals does not always equal 100 (OECD, 1992). In interpreting the ratio for some countries, considerable differences in the total number of men and women must be taken into account. Ratios for some ISCED categories can be explained by the total ratio, or by an inequality of men and women in that age-group. Thus the ratio is not entirely independent of population size. The gender ratio could be improved by using the percentage of people in an ISCED category instead of the "real" number of people. In this way, the ratio of the totals would always equal 100.

The ratio measure is not independent of general educational attainment either. The higher the number of people in an ISCED category, the closer the ratio will come to 100. A surplus of 5 000 men can lead to a ratio of 50 if the ISCED category only contains 10 000 men (and 5 000 women). But if it contains 100 000 men, the ratio is 95. The impact of gender differences varies according to the total number of people in the category, which is not ideal. In some way, however, this differentiation could be justified.

The ratio value for one ISCED category must be seen in the context of ratio values for all the ISCED levels. A high ratio value for one ISCED level in a country may be countered by a low ratio value in another. In other words, what appears to be a satisfactory result in comparing ISCED 3 from the point of view of gender equity may be contrasted by a very different result for ISCED 5/6/7 (Borkowsky and Healy, 1992).

Another problem is the fact that the ratio is limited to a minimum score on one side, but that it is unlimited on the other. In *Education at a Glance* (OECD, 1992), the ratio ranged from 31 (over-representation of men) to 340 (over-representation of women), where a value of 100 stands for equality of educational attainment between the sexes. A direct comparison of scores indicating advantage to men with those indicating advantage to women is impossible. This problem can be solved by taking the difference between the percentages of men and women in a certain ISCED category, and dividing it by the larger of the two. As a consequence, the scores will range between −1 and 1, with 0 being the point of equality (Fossett and South, 1983).

The ratios calculated in *Education at a Glance* (OECD, 1992) give no overall view of the gender differences in a country. Therefore it is not a good indicator. As mentioned before, an indicator must give a single summary measure of inequality.


## 4.    The Dissimilarity Index

For the second edition of *Education at a Glance* (OECD, 1993), the gender ratio for educational attainment was replaced by the dissimilarity index (DI). This index has a long history. Since the 1950s, it has become one of the principal statistics for measuring inequality, and particularly for measuring urban residential segregation by race. Gender differences are often measured by means of the dissimilarity index, but mostly in combination with other variables such as occupational or racial segregation.

The OECD has also used the dissimilarity index to measure occupational gender segregation (OECD, 1985). The use of the DI is not limited to persons. Examples are known where it measures the size of farms or the concentration of words in a text. The DI is used to measure differences between those who have an occupation, an income, a place to live, a diploma, a certain level of education, and those who have not.

The dissimilarity index is the sum of the absolute values of the differences between the percentages of men and women at each level of educational attainment. This sum is divided by two. Although the calculation of the DI may not be as transparent as the gender ratio, the result has concrete meaning. The index shows for each country, in a single measure, the percentage of people who would have to change their level of education in order to bring about similarity in the educational attainment of men and women.

The index is easy to interpret, but it has a few disadvantages. As Theil (1972) also pointed out, the index is not consistent in relation to aggregation. DI increases as the number of ISCED categories increases. The higher the number of ISCED categories upon which the computation is based, the larger will be the expected value of the index. If only three ISCED categories are used instead of four or five, the index becomes smaller for some countries. In other countries the aggregation has no influence on the DI.

However, a more important drawback is that the DI is not suitable for showing differences in gender dissimilarity over time. DI comparisons between the groups of 25 to 34-year-old and 55 to 64-year-old suggest that for some countries there has been no evolution at all, or that gender differences have become larger between the 1960s and the 1990s (*e.g.* in Belgium and Sweden). Applying the definition of the DI, these conclusions are correct. Most readers will take these conclusions for granted, but the reality under-neath these scores shows that sometimes a gender difference in favour of men has changed over time into a gender difference in favour of women. The DI only uses absolute values and ignores the implication of a gender difference in terms of advantages or disadvantages. Therefore, the DI does not meet the criterion of directionality.

The DI gives the percentage of people having to attain another level of education in order to reach equality between men and women, but it does not indicate what level they should attain: the DI does not distinguish between someone who has an ISCED level 2 qualification and should reach ISCED 3, and someone with ISCED 2 who should reach ISCED 6/7. Hence, the interpreter does not receive information on the number and nature of transitions between ISCED levels for men or women.

Authors using the DI for measuring racial-spatial segregation also addressed this weakness, since the DI only shows how many people have to be redistributed so that each area has exactly the same composition as the city as a whole. It gives no indication of how far people have to move. Neither does it allow a distinction to be made between a city where all non-white areas are concentrated into a single ghetto, and a city with dispersed areas of minority residents. White (1983) therefore developed an index of segregation which takes into account spatial structure, *i.e.* the distance between the areas.

A similar index for gender differences could measure the number of people having to change from one ISCED level to the next, counting the number of transitions they have to make. The result would be the percentage of people who have to make one transition (to the next ISCED level). In theory this adjusted dissimilarity index could exceed 100, meaning that everybody has to make at least one transition, and some have to make more.

Table/Tableau 9.1.

**Dissimilarity index (DI) and adjusted dissimilarity index for people 25-34 years of age in New Zealand and Switzerland, 1992**

(Calculations are based on percentage rates)

*Indices de disparité et indices de disparité corrigés pour les personnes âgées de 25 à 34 ans en Nouvelle-Zélande et en Suisse, 1992*

| | New Zealand | | | | |
|---|---|---|---|---|---|
| | Early childhood, primary and lower secondary education ISCED 0/1/2 | Upper secondary education ISCED 3 | Tertiary education, short duration ISCED 5 | Tertiary education, long duration ISCED 6/7 | Sum |
| Men | 35 | 43 | 6 | 14 | 98 |
| Women | 44 | 30 | 14 | 11 | 99 |
| Difference | 9 | 13 | 8 | 3 | DI = 33/2 = 16.5 |
| | 9 | 4 | 3.5 | | |

Number of transitions to be made (adjusted DI) = 9 + 4 + 3.5 = 16.5

| | Switzerland | | | | |
|---|---|---|---|---|---|
| | Early childhood, primary and lower secondary education ISCED 0/1/2 | Upper secondary education ISCED 3 | Tertiary education, short duration ISCED 5 | Tertiary education, long duration ISCED 6/7 | Sum |
| Men | 10 | 60 | 18 | 11 | 99 |
| Women | 15 | 70 | 7 | 6 | 98 |
| Difference | 5 | 10 | 11 | 5 | DI = 31/2 = 15.5 |
| | 5 | 15 | 4.5 | | |

Number of transitions to be made (adjusted DI) = 5 + 15 + 4.5 = 24.5

Several countries would be ranked differently if such an adjusted index were used. This is illustrated in Table 9.1 for New Zealand and Switzerland.

However, even this adjusted dissimilarity index does not show whether more men or more women have to acquire a higher ISCED level in order to reach parity. The adjusted DI, therefore, still does not meet the criterion of directionality.

## 5. The Advantage Index

A new indicator was developed, based on the assumption that the possession of a diploma of tertiary education is an advantage and that people who have not completed upper secondary education are disadvantaged.

130

If the percentage of *men* who do not have a diploma of upper secondary education is higher than the percentage of *women*, then men are disadvantaged. If the percentage of women with a diploma of tertiary education is higher than the percentage of men having a higher diploma, then women are in a position of advantage. Positive index scores indicate that men are advantaged; negative index scores indicate the reverse: that women are advantaged (or men are disadvantaged) (Van de Poele, 1993). As will be shown later, the advantage index (AI) and the adjusted dissimilarity index are related.

The AI in educational achievement is calculated by subtracting the percentage of men in ISCED categories 0/1, 0/1/2, 6/7 and 5/6/7 from the percentage of women in the same categories. The result in category 0/1 is added to the result in category 0/1/2. The result in category 6/7 is added to the result in category 5/6/7. The result of this operation in the higher ISCED levels is subtracted from the result in lower ISCED levels. To obtain an index that in theory ranges from −100 to +100, the result is divided by 4 and multiplied by 100.

This calculation gives the gender differences in the ISCED levels 0/1 and 6/7 a double weight in comparison with the ISCED levels 2 and 5:

−100    means that no man completed lower secondary education and all women have a diploma of tertiary education (university level);

+100    means that no woman completed lower secondary education and all men have a diploma of tertiary education (university level);

0    means that gender differences at the lower ISCED levels are as high as at the higher ISCED levels; 0 does not necessarily mean that there are no gender differences but that advantages compensate disadvantages.

Table 9.2 illustrates how the advantage index is calculated. The formula used differs with the ISCED levels between which countries differentiate in the delivered data. For the third edition of *Education at a Glance* (OECD, 1995), half of the countries presented data for all ISCED levels. For these countries the full formula can be used. Seven countries did not make a distinction between the levels 0/1 and 2. Only four countries delivered one category for all types of tertiary education. For some countries, a combination of the full and the short formula had to be used.

At first, the DI and the AI were both calculated with only three ISCED categories: 0/1/2, 3 and 5/6/7. For both indices, it became clear that the formulas had to be changed in such a way that gender differences in, for example, ISCED 5 were counted differently from differences in ISCED 6/7. It was assumed that part of the advantaged situation of women in most countries could be attributed more to differences in ISCED 5 than in ISCED 6/7. For the younger age-groups, the aggregation of the ISCED levels 0/1 and 2 is acceptable. The lower ISCED levels should be taken into the calculation separately if changes over time are to be presented, since in the older age-groups the gender differences can give a different picture in ISCED 0/1 and ISCED 2. For some countries, Belgium for example, the full and the short formula result in quite different index scores.

ISCED 3 data are not used in the formula for the advantage index. Thus the variations in ISCED 3 are not directly taken into account for this indicator, but the variation in ISCED 3 is the reflection of the gender differences in the other categories. If

Table/Tableau 9.2.

**Calculation of the advantage index**

(Calculations are based on percentage rates)

*Calcul de l'indice d'avantage fondé sur des pourcentages*

| | Early childhood and primary education ISCED 0/1 | Lower secondary education ISCED 2 | Upper secondary education ISCED 3 | Tertiary education (non university) ISCED 5 | Tertiary education (university) ISCED 6/7 | Sum |
|---|---|---|---|---|---|---|
| Men | 24 | 12 | 43 | 7 | 14 | 100 |
| Women | 26 | 18 | 30 | 14 | 12 | 100 |

| | | | | | | |
|---|---|---|---|---|---|---|
| 24 | | └────────── 76 ──────────┘ | | | | |
| 2 | | | | | | |
| 26 | | 74 | | | | |

More women than men have not attained lower secondary education: advantage for men + 2

| | | | | | | |
|---|---|---|---|---|---|---|
| 36 | | 64 | | | | |
| 8 | | | | | | |
| 44 | | 56 | | | | |

More women than men have not attained lower secondary education: advantage for men + 8

| | | | | | | |
|---|---|---|---|---|---|---|
| 79 | | 21 | | | | |
| –5 | | | | | | |
| 74 | | 26 | | | | |

More women than men have attained higher education: disadvantage for men – 5

| | | | | | | |
|---|---|---|---|---|---|---|
| 86 | | 14 | | | | |
| 2 | | | | | | |
| 88 | | 12 | | | | |

More men than women have attained higher education of university level: advantage for men + 2
Calculation of the index: + 2 + 8 – 5 + 2 = 7/4 = 1.75

there are more men than women in ISCED 3, this could indicate an advantage as well as a disadvantage, depending on what the gender differences look like in the other categories. When men and women are equally represented at a lower educational level, an over-representation of men in ISCED 3 is a disadvantage because this automatically means that fewer men have a diploma of tertiary education. Thus, variation in ISCED 3 is included indirectly in the calculations, and not using ISCED 3 in the formula does not result in omission of a part of the data.

The advantage of having completed upper secondary education is regarded as representing the same value as the advantage of having a diploma of tertiary education. A disadvantage-point (%) in ISCED 0/1/2 is considered the equivalent of an advantage-point (%) in ISCED 5/6/7 and *vice versa*. There is no proof that this is the case in all countries. Nevertheless, the adjusted dissimilarity index also has to deal with more or less the same value problem: for example, if the DI index shows that 10 per cent of the people have to change one ISCED level, this could mean that 5 per cent have to change from ISCED 2 to ISCED 3 (or *vice versa*), and another 5 per cent from ISCED 3 to ISCED 5/6/7 (or *vice versa*). Although the number of people that have to change is the same, this can hardly be said of the effort that it would take to achieve that change. The problem of unequal intervals is thus not a problem unique to the advantage index.

The AI is a composite of (dis)advantage scores in the lower and higher educational categories. In half of the countries, an advantage for men or women works in the same direction in the lower educational categories as in the higher ones. For example, if in these countries there are fewer women than men with lower levels of education (which means an advantage for women), women will also be advantaged by being more highly educated, or *vice versa*. Nevertheless, in the other countries, advantages for men or women work in opposite directions. This can result in an overall equality according to the index. A zero score does not mean that there are no gender differences, but that they are compensated. The index may also conceal certain gender differences since no distinction is made between different branches in secondary education. In fact, women often choose subjects or courses that offer distinct professional career opportunities.

The advantage index looks less transparent than the dissimilarity index when it comes to interpretation. The AI scores may be more meaningful if there is agreement to work with an index that is not limited to −100 to +100, and to accept a range from −400 to +400 (the result of not dividing the index by 4). In that case, the AI could be interpreted as the difference between the percentage of men and the percentage of women who have to attain the next ISCED level in order to reach similarity in educational attainment, under the condition that only changes for the better (to a higher ISCED level) are allowed. This interpretation of the AI shows the relation between the advantage index and the adjusted dissimilarity index, which can be illustrated by comparing the way in which the two indices are calculated. This is done in Table 9.3. Nevertheless, the DI is easier to comprehend than the AI. That is the price to be paid for the additional information on directionality in AI.

Table/Tableau 9.3.

**Relation between the advantage index (AI) and the adjusted dissimilarity index (%)**

*Rapport entre l'indice d'avantage et l'indice de disparité corrigé (%)*

|  | Early childhood and primary education ISCED 0/1 | Lower secondary education ISCED 2 | Upper secondary education ISCED 3 | Tertiary education, short duration ISCED 5 | Tertiary education, long duration ISCED 6/7 | Sum |
|---|---|---|---|---|---|---|
| Men | 24 | 12 | 43 | 7 | 14 | 100 |
| Women | 26 | 18 | 30 | 14 | 12 | 100 |

Adjusted dissimilarity index: 2 + 8 + 5 + 2 = 17
Advantage index: 2 + 8 - 5 + 2 = + 7 (7/4 = + 1.75)

The advantage index and the adjusted dissimilarity index are both measures of ordinal inequality. The ordinary dissimilarity index, by contrast, is a measure of nominal differentiation.

## 6.  The Years of Schooling Index

A last index that was considered within Network B measures the average duration of formal education in years for men and women. By dividing the average number for women by the average number for men (and multiplying it by 100), one obtains a ratio with 100 as the point of equality (below 100 means an advantage for men; above 100 an advantage for women). The index shows whether the average number of years of schooling is similar among men and women. Since at an international level, there are no available data sources on the duration of education of individual respondents, this has to be estimated on the basis of the number of years of schooling required to complete each ISCED level. These numbers are multiplied by the number of men and women at these ISCED levels. The most vulnerable element in this calculation is the decision on how many years of schooling should be allotted to each ISCED category in each country. In Network B, country representatives were asked to make this decision after national deliberation. The weight given to an ISCED category differs from country to country. The method used in calculating the index of years of schooling is illustrated in Table 9.4.

The index of years of schooling is not independent of the general educational attainment level. Higher education is given a higher weight than lower education. This

Table / Tableau 9.4.

**Calculation of the index of years of schooling**

*Calcul de l'indice d'années de scolarité (%)*

|  | Early childhood and primary education ISCED 0/1 | Lower secondary education ISCED 2 | Upper secondary education ISCED 3 | Tertiary education, short duration ISCED 5 | Tertiary education, long duration ISCED 6/7 | Sum |
|---|---|---|---|---|---|---|
| Men | 24 | 12 | 43 | 7 | 14 | 100 |
| Women | 26 | 18 | 30 | 14 | 12 | 100 |
| Required number of years | 6 | 10 | 12 | 16 | 18 | |
| Calculation | | | | | | |
| Men | 144 | 120 | 516 | 112 | 252 | 1 144 |
| Women | 156 | 180 | 360 | 224 | 216 | 1 136 |
| | | | | | | 1 136/1 144 = 0.99 (x 100) |

can easily be accepted if one aims at measuring educational attainment. Although Chart C2B in *Education at a Glance* (OECD, 1993) showed that gender similarity is more characteristic in countries with a relatively high and a relatively low educational attainment, an index of gender differences should be constant in relation to the general educational attainment of the population.

In the index of years of schooling, gender differences in favour of women are overestimated in countries having a low general level of educational attainment, compared with countries having a high level of educational attainment. This is due to the mathematical fact that the difference between the numerator and the denominator has less influence on the result of a division when the numerator and denominator become larger. This is the case for countries with a high level of educational attainment.

ISCED categories are often interpreted differently in different countries. The transformation of the ISCED categories into the number of years of schooling comes closer to the real national situations than the distribution of people over ISCED categories. However, one should bear in mind that the risk of multiplication of errors still exists, since the ISCED distribution as well as the chosen theoretical number of years for each ISCED category, is based on samples and estimations.

The imbalance of the index scores on both sides of the point of equality (100), as was mentioned for the ratio values, occurs here as well. Furthermore, not only the maximum scores below and above 100 are different, they also differ according to the theoretical number of years a country has chosen. In one country (ISCED 0/1 = 6 years; ISCED 6/7 = 17 years) the extreme values can be 35 and 283, while in another country (ISCED 0/1 = 5 years; ISCED 6/7 = 18 years) they are 28 and 360.

Although these irregularities are serious drawbacks if one aims at a rationally normalised measure, the influence on the ranking of OECD countries is small since general educational attainment and educational structures in these countries are not that different. The output of the index of years of schooling and the advantage index are similar.

Table / Tableau 9.5.

**Summary of whether the indices satisfy the proposed criteria**

*Correspondance entre les indices et les critères proposés*

|  | General attainment invariance | Directionality | Concrete meaning | Organisation invariance | Size invariance | Rational normalisation |
|---|---|---|---|---|---|---|
| Ratio | − | + | − | − | − | − |
| Adjusted ratio | − | + | − | − | + | + |
| Dissimilarity | + | − | + | − | + | + |
| Adjusted dissimilarity | + | − | + | − | + | + |
| Advantage | + | + | − + | − | + | + |
| Number of years | − | + | + | − | + | − |

135

## 7. Conclusion

How to measure gender differences in educational attainment was one of the most intensively discussed issues in Network B. This resulted in a different index in each of the first three editions of *Education at a Glance*. No doubt the DI and the AI are better indicators than the gender ratios. There are differences in the quality of the indices as well as in the information they provide. However, none of the indices meets all the criteria suggested at the beginning of this chapter, as is shown in Table 9.5.

The gender ratio can very easily be calculated, but it does not provide a single measure for gender differences. The dissimilarity index has a concrete meaning, but gives no information on which gender is favoured in educational attainment, and is misleading when different age-groups are compared. The advantage index is less easy to interpret but it gives additional information on directionality. The index of years of schooling is very promising since it offers a solution to the omnipresent problem of ISCED interpretation, provided that there is a limited range of general educational attainment in the countries compared.

# References

BONCKAERT, P. and EGGHE, L. (1991), "Rational normalization of concentration measures", *Journal of the American Society for Information Science*, No. 42 (10), pp. 715-722.

BORKOWSKY, A. and HEALY, T. (1992), "Report on the development of C2 for Education at a Glance, 1994", unpublished paper written for the OECD INES project, OECD, Paris.

FOSSETT, M. and SOUTH, J.S. (1983), "The measurement of intergroup income inequality: a conceptual review", *Social Forces*, No. 61 (3), pp. 855-871.

FOSSETT, M.A., GALLE, O.R., and KELLY, W.R. (1986), "Racial occupational inequality, 1940-1980: national and regional trends", *American Sociological Review*, No. 88 (3), pp. 421-429.

MERSCHROD, K. (1981), "The index of dissimilarity as a measure of inequality", *Quality and Quantity*, No. 15 (4), pp. 403-411.

OECD (1985), *The Integration of Women into the Economy*, Paris.

OECD (1992), *Education at a Glance: OECD Indicators* (bilingual), 1st edition, CERI, Paris.

OECD (1993), *Education at a Glance: OECD Indicators* (bilingual), 2nd edition, CERI, Paris.

OECD (1995), *Education at a Glance: OECD Indicators*, 3rd edition, CERI, Paris.

THEIL, H. (1972), *Statistical Decomposition Analysis*, North Holland Press, Amsterdam.

VAN DE POELE, L. (1993), "Leerplicht en scholingsgraad" (Compulsory education and educational attainment), *Tijdschrift voor Onderwijsrecht en Onderwijsbeleid*, Vol. 4 (2), pp. 88-93.

WATTS, M. (1992), "How should occupational sex segregation be measured?", *Work, Employment and Society*, Vol. 6 (3), pp. 475-487.

WHITE, M.J. (1983), "The measurement of spatial segregation", *American Journal of Sociology*, No. 88 (3), pp. 1008-1018.

# Indicators of Continuing Education and Training
## *Indicateurs de la formation continue*

*by*

**Anna Borkowsky**
Federal Office of Statistics, Bern, Switzerland
**Maurice van der Heiden**
Ministry of Education, Culture and Science, Zoetermeer, the Netherlands
*and*
**Albert Tuijnman**
OECD Secretariat, Paris, France

This chapter opens with a discussion of the policy contexts and orientations of continuing education and training in the perspective of the lifelong learning society. Lifelong learning is not a vague and utopian idea, but an inevitable reality for the future development of education systems in the OECD countries. Attention is paid to the need to develop indicators in the domain of continuing education and training, and examples are given of areas for which indicators of relevance to policy-making might be developed. It is then demonstrated that it is feasible to measure at least some aspects of continuing education and training using available data sources, such as the regular labour force surveys. An analysis of the data first collected for the third edition of *Education at a Glance* (OECD, 1995) is also presented. It is concluded that the time has now come to take seriously the challenge of developing quantitative measures of continuing education and training, both nationally and internationally.

\*

\*    \*

# Note de synthèse

*Ce chapitre s'ouvre sur une analyse des politiques gouvernementales dans lesquelles s'inscrit la formation continue, et de ses orientations dans la perspective d'une culture d'apprentissage permanent. L'éducation permanente n'est pas présentée comme un concept vague et utopique, mais comme une réalité incontournable pour le développement futur des systèmes d'éducation des pays Membres de l'OCDE.*

*Les auteurs soulignent la nécessité de mettre au point des indicateurs relatifs à la formation continue et donnent des exemples de domaines dans lesquels il serait possible de construire des indicateurs utiles aux décideurs. Ils font une première distinction entre la formation continue en tant qu'investissement et la formation en vue d'un épanouissement personnel. Une autre distinction est établie entre la formation liée à l'emploi et la formation liée aux loisirs. Parmi les exemples de domaines pour lesquels des indicateurs sont proposés, les auteurs mentionnent les coûts de la formation continue et les dépenses qui lui sont consacrées, la durée des programmes, les types de prestataires, le volume total d'inscriptions, les qualifications obtenues à la faveur d'une formation continue et le rendement d'un investissement dans une formation complémentaire qualifiante pour l'individu et la société.*

*Les auteurs montrent qu'il est possible de mesurer au moins certains aspects de la formation continue en faisant appel aux sources de données disponibles, comme les enquêtes régulières sur la population active. Ils analysent en outre le premier indicateur de formation continue présenté à titre liminaire dans la troisième édition de* Regards sur l'éducation *(OCDE, 1995). Ils concluent en faisant observer que le moment est venu de relever le défi que constitue l'élaboration d'indicateurs quantitatifs de la formation continue à l'échelon national et international.*

\*

\*    \*

## 1.    The Changing Policy Context

Continuing education and training (CET) have an important role to play in promoting economic growth and, more generally, enhancing the development of society. The role of CET is closely tied to technological development, the globalisation of the economy, and high unemployment in many OECD countries. The imperative of improving workers' productivity in order to maintain competitiveness in a global economy provides a strong rationale for investment in CET. Efforts in this direction will need to grow as technological change accelerates.

In the new situation, special tasks are emerging for continuing education and training. These relate to economic and social objectives, to which CET is expected to contribute. Among the economic objectives are those of improving the efficiency, productivity and profitability of the work organisation and hence of raising individual earnings and, eventually, national income. Other goals concern the prevention of skills obsolescence and the alleviation of redundancy pressure among the various high-risk groups in an industrial society, especially the initially poorly educated and those with a comparatively weak attachment to the labour market: women, older employees and workers employed in labour markets undergoing rationalisation and "structural adjustment". Additional goals for CET are to improve the employability of displaced people and school leavers lacking adequate prospects for an occupational career and, of course, to satisfy the social demand for education. At an individual level, the objectives relate not merely to economics but also to a large extent to social psychology: the satisfaction of individual demand is not just a matter of meeting material needs or even perceived learning needs, but also concerns higher-order needs in relation to subjective well-being and satisfaction with life – something which, in the 1970s, led some economists to hypothesise that adult education was less an investment than a consumption good, a pastime of the already to an extent "over-educated" middle classes.

The policy context of continuing education and training has changed remarkably since the mid-1980s. Increasingly, the tendency has been to strengthen informal learning in the workplace and in other life settings. In some countries this has implied reducing the size of formal, institution-based adult education, which was at the heart of policies for the development of continuing education during the 1960s and 1970s. A concomitant development is the shift away from the role of government in finance and provision and towards an emphasis on the responsibility of the social partners and the individual adult learner. The new policy context is well described by the notion of the "training market". In such a market, the matching of learning demand to the supply of opportunities is left to forces other than those associated with government regulations. Even though genuine "markets" for learning do not exist in the OECD countries, it is nevertheless widely believed that a market approach offers a means of reducing the need for public intervention, broadening the supply of learning opportunities, strengthening the perceived relevance of the provision, and improving quality while reducing costs.

The above concerns call attention to the imperative of developing the lifelong learning society. The objectives associated with lifelong learning are most likely to be achieved if learning becomes an essential ingredient and condition of both work and leisure. Learning should take place not only within the walls of educational institutions, but increasingly also in the workplace and at home. As a consequence of rapid technological, social and economic change, education and training can no longer be the preserve of the young. This context of lifelong learning sets the background for major policy issues, such as decisions about the orientation of continuing education and training in terms of target audiences, contents, and the role of governments in finance and provision, the means of influencing the demand and supply of learning opportunities for adults, and the extent to which individuals, firms, and governments should share in the financing of supply. These questions are given new significance as a consequence of the *OECD Jobs Study* (OECD, 1994), in which it is recommended that lifelong learning should feature centrally in a high-productivity, high-wage strategy for job creation.

## 2. The Orientation of Continuing Education and Training (CET)

There are two main roles for CET. The first concerns skills training for either the present job or a future occupation. The second important role of CET lies outside the world of work. Examples are education directed at cultural participation and social competence, and education for personal development and growth. These two perspectives are variously called "training for investment" and "training for consumption", thereby clearly indicating the theoretical framework within which this distinction may be placed, namely that of human capital theory.

Although CET also plays an important role outside the world of work, many governments give priority to the labour-market functions of CET. This emphasis on training for investment reflects a belief in the increasing importance of knowledge as a primary factor in the production of goods and services. Knowledge is society's main resource. It must be kept up to standard and developed further through lifelong learning, on the basis of sound foundation skills acquired through initial schooling.

Increasing the supply of skilled workers and reducing unemployment is a central goal. The unemployed, and workers facing redundancy as a consequence of structural adjustment, are therefore among the primary target groups for CET. In the OECD countries it may be expected that the long-term unemployed workers who claim social security benefits will increasingly be required to participate in job training programmes that are tailored as closely as possible to this group's needs. The main purpose will be to "help the unemployed to help themselves", by requiring them to upgrade their skills.

Women constitute a second important audience for CET. In all OECD countries, female labour force participation rates are traditionally lower than those of men, and women are often employed part-time or have temporary, low-skill jobs demanding irregular working hours. Consequently, many countries target CET provision so as to enhance the opportunities of women to enter stable, high-skill jobs.

School drop-outs form a third priority group for CET provision. Even if young people lacking adequate qualifications manage to enter into employment, they still face a higher than average risk of becoming unemployed. The training effort that would then be required is often greater than would have been the case had they completed an educational programme to begin with. Ensuring that all young people obtain a basic qualification is therefore a priority of government policy.

The trend towards multiculturalism and the arrival in many OECD countries of large numbers of immigrants places another demand on CET. Immigrants who stay in a host country for prolonged periods of time, whether by choice or necessity, have in principle the right to play a full part in the development of that society. Often, however, they lack the means and skills to do so, whether these be literacy skills or the vocational qualifications required by employers. Societies thus have a duty to ensure that the conditions for integration exist. Again, CET can be an important instrument in this respect.

Developments in the world of work are closely linked with the development of leisure. In recent decades, the individual's working life has increasingly been concentrated between the ages of 20 and 60. People between these ages generally have little time for leisure, whereas those over 60 or 65 tend to have more free time. This development has created a strong demand for CET among senior citizens, for whom education is an important means to several ends, for example, keeping abreast of the rapid changes taking place in the world around them – from the advent of cashpoints and new medical techniques to the spread of the values and norms of other cultures.

CET for consumption is no less crucial to the development of society than CET for investment, and getting more people into employment is not only an economic goal. Many other aspects of social participation and personal development are also at stake, both in and beyond the world of paid work. For example, the distribution of work is closely linked with the distribution of wealth, social participation and psychological well-being. In this respect, a policy aimed at job creation complements a policy aimed at promoting equal opportunities in education, since unemployment and inactivity correlate positively with age and inversely with educational attainment.

The contribution of CET to personal development and growth must not be underestimated. The reference here is less to on-the-job training or publicly sponsored training programmes and more to "traditional" or "liberal" adult education, such as the learning activities of the study circles and folkhögskolor sponsored by the popular educational associations in the Nordic countries, adult basic and secondary education in the Netherlands, or the community colleges in North America. The provision of liberal adult education can be expected to grow in importance as the OECD societies become more knowledge-intensive. One factor is that the technological revolution has added new techniques to the traditional methods of teaching and learning. That new information technologies have changed the premises of the lifelong learning society is beyond question, and the education system will need to respond accordingly.

It is not only the workplace in the OECD countries which has become more knowledge-intensive and information-intensive, but also the wider civic and political society, thereby making it more difficult to understand political issues and raising the barriers to political participation. A well-informed citizenry is crucial in maintaining and strengthening democratic institutions in the OECD countries. There is a role for CET in achieving the aim of having an informed citizenry.

However, given the uncertainties, the notion of the "learning society" is not entirely unambiguous. As currently understood, it cannot be used to guide policy in a direct sense. What is clear, however, is that governments can steer the development of the markets for CET only to a limited extent. The "learning society" is not something that can be captured in institutions and policy papers; what people do, whether or not with the help of the new information technologies, has a dynamic force of its own.

## 3.   Why Develop CET Indicators?

If CET is becoming increasingly important as an economic, social and cultural factor, as is argued above, then it is important that knowledge of CET markets should be developed. If an effective policy for CET is to be devised, it will be necessary to establish answers to questions such as where existing CET provision needs to be modified, improved and extended; and how these changes can best be achieved. Unfortunately, this cannot be properly done without comprehensive data, which are generally lacking in most OECD countries.

Both research studies and work in policy analysis can contribute to the development of a knowledge base for CET. Statistics and indicators form a part of the required knowledge base as well. Detailed statistical information is required to monitor trends and developments at the national level. Multiple indicators – and hence multiple information sources – are needed for the monitoring of developments in this domain of educational provision (Tuijnman, 1987).

At the national level, statistics and indicators of the adult education market can be derived from sample surveys or from the administrative records kept by the institutions offering adult education, the central statistical offices and other government agencies. However, information is also needed at the international level. Comparative indicators of key aspects of the system for CET provision – for example, in terms of finance, provision and outcomes – can offer an external framework of reference. Such a framework may allow the decision-makers and others to assign meaning to national trends, and to evaluate the results in a broad international perspective. Thus, in summary, comparative analysis is needed to determine whether the levels of investment and participation in CET, the quality of programme offerings, and the results achieved are adequate in the light of both national goals and international standards.

## 4.  Previous and On-going Work on Training Statistics

In 1988, recognition of the importance of CET for individuals, employers and nations led the OECD Member countries to adopt a programme of work committing the Organisation to undertaking studies in three related areas: 1) the educational attainment of the labour force; 2) the patterns of investment in the skill formation process; and 3) the functioning of training markets and the role therein of collective bargaining and the certification of skills and competencies. These studies, which were conducted between 1988 and 1992 (*cf.* OECD, 1991*a*; OECD, 1993), provided a valuable understanding mainly of the inputs into CET markets, for example, the size of these markets in terms of investment and participation. Some insights into the functioning of CET markets were also obtained, for example, in relation to skills shortages and the skill formation process.

In parallel with the above programme of work, the OECD also appointed a group of National Experts on Training Statistics, which reports to both the Education Committee and the Employment, Labour and Social Affairs Committee. The expert group began its work in 1989, and delivered its first report two years later (OECD, 1991*b*). The purpose was to prepare a training statistics manual that would provide a conceptual framework linking training inputs (costs and volume) to training processes and structural outcomes. The manual would, moreover, clarify methodological issues associated with the collection of comparable statistics about CET at the international level. As a part of this work, the different national strategies for CET data collection were studied, and the applied definitions and methodologies carefully scrutinised.

A draft training statistics manual (unpublished) deals with issues in the measurement of CET. It is stated that the main problem besetting operationalisation and measurement is the lack of consistency in the definitions of CET used by the countries:

"Current definitions of training are often confusing, poorly understood and restrictive. Part of the problem is the failure of these definitions to recognise that training is a pervasive, diverse, diffuse and, in many instances, an extremely nebulous activity. Thus, simple definitions of training are prone to misinterpretation, since they fail to explicate the specific gamut of the training activities involved, while more comprehensive definitions tend to obfuscate by their complexity. Another major problem presented by the measurement of training is that of delineation which, because of the fine distinctions involved, is not easy to resolve. There are four major aspects to this problem. These are the difficulties of distinguishing: *i)* training from non-training activities, *e.g.,* distinguishing training from output, consumption, etc.; *ii)* one type of training activity from another type, *e.g.,* initial from continuing training, specific from general training, etc.; *iii)* one training process from another, *e.g.,* learning by being informed from learning by being shown how to perform a task by someone who is physically present; and *iv)* the particular structural forms of given training processes."

The OECD programme of work on the development of a conceptual and methodological basis for CET statistics is still on-going. A series of technical consultations will be held in 1995 to discuss and revise the draft manual, and to improve the transparency of training statistics by achieving agreement among the countries on taxonomies and survey methods.

## 5. What CET Indicators Might be Proposed?

In the above, several passing remarks were made about the policy areas for which indicators might be developed. The following areas stand out as particularly important:

- cost, expenditure and finance;
- CET duration;
- types of CET provider;
- volume of participation;
- learner appraisal and the recognition of skills and competencies; and
- the individual and social returns to investments in CET.

### Cost, Expenditure and Finance

In order to obtain a complete picture of the education and training effort of the OECD countries, measures of both public and private expenditure on CET must be developed and the data combined with estimates of total public and private expenditure on formal education. Whereas in the latter area much progress has been made, knowledge about the level of expenditure on CET is totally inadequate. This is partly due to the fact that there is no agreement on what should be included in CET cost estimates, which are a compound of many factors, *e.g.* labour, materials, equipment, opportunity costs, etc. Information is required not only about costs and expenditures for CET, but also about the strategies used to finance CET. It would be important to know the sources of the funds spent on CET.

## *Duration*

Duration is an important variable in CET, partly because in the absence of more direct information, it is used as a proxy for training intensity. Duration is of course also a major factor in the cost of CET programmes.

## *Providers*

Countries would want to know what institutions and agencies provide CET, of what types, at what costs, and with what results. In the Netherlands, for example, adult education is provided by four types of institution: 1) those delivering courses which are wholly or largely maintained by the central government; 2) accredited institutions; 3) approved institutions; and 4) private institutions which have not sought government approval (Netherlands Ministry of Education and Science, 1993; Netherlands Ministry of Social Affairs and Employment, 1991). Some of these institutions grant diplomas and certificates that carry equivalency in the formal sector, whereas others are not entitled to do this. There are important differences between these types of institution also with respect to the mixture of public and private funding, whether or not they operate for profit, the means of quality assurance, and the results they achieve. For the OECD countries it would certainly be of interest to know the shares of the different types of provider in total provision, to compare these with the stated policies in respect to the relative weights of the private "training market" and the government-regulated sector of CET, and to develop some kind of measure of the effectiveness of the mixture in a particular country.

## *Participation*

An indicator of the total volume of participation in CET would be of interest to policy-makers, although it would not offer insights into the specificities of the volume and mode of functioning of CET markets, given the highly diversified structures that characterise CET provision in all OECD countries. Therefore, once the overall level of participation in any given reference period is established, it would be necessary to determine the orientation of the programmes in which the learners participate. As was mentioned in a previous section, it is necessary to make a distinction between CET for investment and CET for consumption, even though such a distinction might pose conceptual and measurement problems. Another classification could be based on the characteristics of the participants. Age, sex, previous educational attainment, socio-economic status, employment status, immigrant status, etc., are all relevant variables in this respect.

## Appraisal and Certification

The CET market encompasses a very wide and varied range of courses and qualifications. That variety is functional, since it enables the market to respond in different ways to the learning needs and aspirations of individual participants, both in the world of work and in other fields. However, this fragmentation also has certain drawbacks. For example, adult learners often cannot obtain unambiguous information on the nature and value of the opportunities on offer in the CET market. This is also a drawback from the viewpoint of employers, who cannot easily assess the worth of CET programmes. For the CET providers themselves, it is often difficult to assess what knowledge and skills prospective participants already possess, limiting the scope for customised provision.

To overcome these problems, procedures are needed for the validation of knowledge and skills acquired outside the mainstream system of education with its emphasis on formal qualifications. This is why certain OECD countries – for example, Australia, France, the Netherlands, New Zealand and the United Kingdom – have taken steps to create an assessment system that evaluates and certifies adults' skills and competence in particular occupational fields or subjects.

The OECD's indicators on the level of educational attainment of the adult population are based only on the qualifications obtained in the system of formal, initial education; the qualifications people obtain through participation in CET are mostly not included. However, as CET becomes more important socially and economically, and as CET markets develop and expand in relation to increases in the demand for learning opportunities, it will eventually become necessary to take account of CET in education statistics. It will thus become necessary to establish the formal equivalency levels of certain CET programmes, so that the full picture can be taken into account in measuring an indicator such as that of the educational attainment of the population.

## Individual and Social Returns to CET

Finally, it would be necessary to develop indicators of the individual and social returns to CET investments, both absolute and relative to the rate of return to an investment in upper secondary and tertiary education. Information about the returns is needed in order to clarify the investment options. The information may also be used to determine how the cost of CET should be shared among the principal stakeholders – individual participants, firms and the whole society.

## 6. The Development of CET Indicators

The development of CET indicators within the INES framework was left to Network B, the network which occupies itself with the relationship and transitions between education and the labour market. Given the traditions of the network and the expertise of its members, it was natural that the group would seek to establish indicators using existing data from surveys of individuals, either the labour market surveys used in other indicators developed by the network or other specialised household surveys.

According to the network's template, the indicator "Continuing Education and Training for Adults" is part of the "Participation and Flows" element of the domain on "Educational Programmes and Processes". The main purpose of the indicator is therefore to complement the information on participation in the formal education system, so that a better picture of the whole educational effort of a given country can be obtained. In this broad sense, there is no need to distinguish *a priori* between the different orientations and types of CET, or between the possible different functions of CET.

The definition according to the template is as follows:

"Continuing education and training for adults refers to all kinds of general and job-related education and training organised, financed or sponsored by public authorities, provided by employers or self-financed.

Job-related continuing education and training refers to all organised, systematic education and training activities in which people take part in order to obtain knowledge and/or to learn new skills for their current or future jobs, to increase earnings, to improve job and/or career opportunities in their current or another field, and generally to improve their opportunities for advancement and promotion.

Continuing education and training for adults does not include military training or full-time studies at level 5/6/7 according to ISCED."

By defining CET as a "systematic, organised (...) activity in which people take part in order to obtain knowledge (...)" the template makes use of the basic elements of the definition of the formal education system used in ISCED. With this definition, learning activities are to be considered part of CET only if they are set apart as such and involve people in the formal roles of teacher and learner. Much of the on-going process of acquiring new skills and knowledge informally, on the job, is therefore excluded. This important domain of adult learning should be considered in further work.

The template also distinguishes job-related from other kinds of CET. The wording used in the template points to the qualification or upgrading of the labour force as the main function of CET. "Job-related" is defined in a very wide sense, the only effective requirement for classifying a given activity as job-related being the subjective assessment of the individual. The template then defines the rate of participation in job-related CET for the whole population and for the employed population only. The data for the first indicator on CET published in the third edition of *Education at a Glance* (OECD, 1995) was collected for the employed population only.

## 7. Preliminary Results

In 1994, the INES project for the first time collected data for an indicator on the volume of participation in CET. The data were collected in accordance with the requirements set out in the above templates. A first indicator of CET participation was included in *Education at a Glance* (OECD, 1995). The indicator showed the participation by the employed population in job-related CET.

Figure 10.1 shows substantial variation in the overall participation rates of the employed in job-related CET, with a spread of nearly 20 percentage points between the countries with the highest and the lowest yearly participation rates. These differences should be interpreted with caution. At the present stage of the developmental work it is still unclear how much of the differences in participation rates is genuine and how much is due to differences in the way in which questions are asked and in the definitions that are applied.

Figure 10.2 presents a breakdown of job-related CET participation by levels of initial educational attainment. This indicator shows clearly that participation in job-related CET is closely related to the previously attained level of education. In all countries that supplied data, CET participants with the lowest levels of educational attainment also show the lowest CET participation rates, whereas those with a tertiary level of education show the highest participation rates. In nearly all OECD countries, participation in job-related CET is highest among those with university education, although in France, persons with a non-university tertiary education are the most frequent participants. The participation rates in job-related CET for holders of university degrees are at least twice as high as those of persons with primary or lower secondary education in all OECD countries, the ratio going up to five times higher in some countries.

Figure 10.3 shows a breakdown of participation in job-related CET by age. It can be seen from the results that, with the exception of Sweden, participation declines with age, with an especially sharp drop for the oldest group (45-64 years).

Figure 10.4 shows the participation in job-related CET of the employed population for men and women separately. There is remarkably little difference in the overall participation rates between the sexes. With the exception of Switzerland, marginally more women than men participate.

In conclusion, the data would appear to establish clearly that the higher participation rates of the better educated are found in all age-groups and among both sexes, in all OECD countries.

## 8. Some Critical Observations

The data used to measure the above indicators on CET are mostly derived from the national labour force surveys. One problem is that different countries use different reference periods, with the countries falling into two main groups: some European Union countries, using a four-week period, and the North American countries with a one-year reference period. All countries which provided data from special surveys used the one-year reference period. The results obtained with the two reference periods are not comparable. A split presentation of the data is therefore necessary. On the whole, a one-year reference period seems preferable.

Figure/*Graphique* 10.1. **Participation in job-related continuing education and training
for the employed population**
*Participation à la formation continue liée à l'emploi, destinée aux actifs occupés*

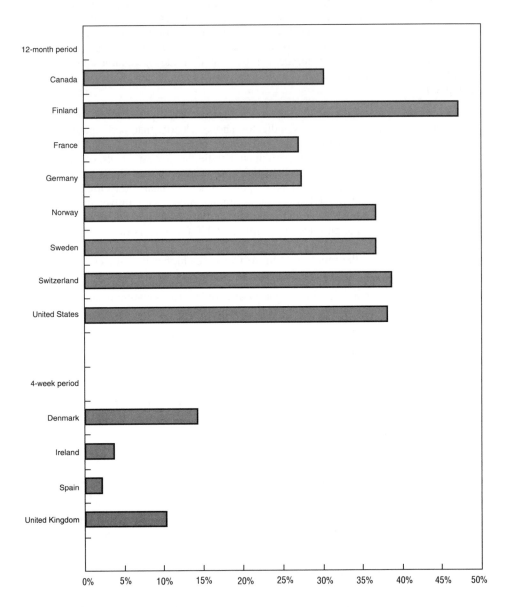

*Source:* From OECD data.

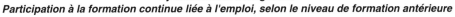

Figure/*Graphique* 10.2. **Participation in job-related continuing education and training**
**by educational background**
*Participation à la formation continue liée à l'emploi, selon le niveau de formation antérieure*

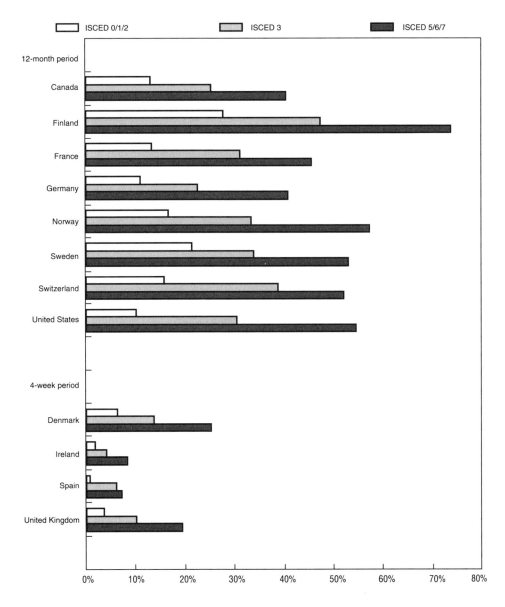

*Source:* From OECD data.

151

Figure/*Graphique* 10.3. **Participation in job-related continuing education and training by age**
*Participation à la formation continue liée à l'emploi selon l'âge*

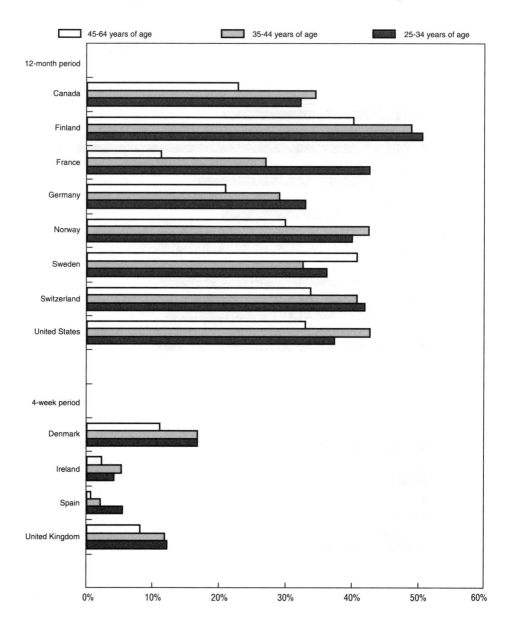

*Source:* From OECD data.

152

Figure/*Graphique* 10.4.   **Participation in job-related continuing education and training by gender**
*Participation à la formation continue liée à l'emploi selon le sexe*

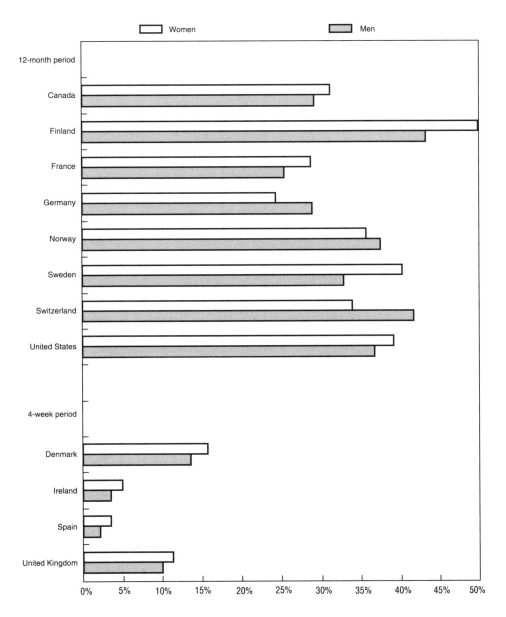

*Source:*   From OECD data.

There is some doubt whether the applications of the definitions of job-related CET are the same for all countries. In Germany, for instance, courses of short duration are excluded from consideration during the interview, while in Switzerland there are no restrictions such as a minimum duration of CET activities. The consequences of these seemingly minor differences need to be explored further.

## 9.   Proposed Further Work on CET Indicators

Among the variety of relevant policy areas for which further indicators might be developed, some appear particularly important. For pragmatic reasons, the work will have to concentrate on areas where results are to be expected in the foreseeable future. The further development of CET indicators will concentrate on the following areas: duration of CET, the social background of the participants, the characteristics of the providers of CET, and institutional statistics.

### *Duration of CET*

Given the fact that CET is organised in widely differing ways throughout the OECD countries and takes varying amounts of time, the final part of the CET template suggests weighting the participation rates by the amount of time spent in CET. Discussion will have to take place about possible ways of measuring the time spent on CET. Possibilities include distinguishing between several categories of duration, for example, between courses longer and shorter than one month or six months, and/or taking into account the weekly time spent on a given course. Careful consideration will also have to be given to the question whether only the time spent in class or on the learning task should be included, or the time spent doing homework for CET should be added.

### *Social Background of Participants*

Given that the purpose of an indicator on CET is to complement the INES indicators on participation and flows, it would be logical to develop a CET indicator for the entire adult population, and not, as was done this first time, solely for the employed population.

One further step might be to obtain breakdowns of the CET indicator not only by age, gender, initial educational attainment and employment status, but also by social background and employment sector.

In the opening sections of this chapter, a description was offered of the orientations of CET according to certain population groups with specific learning needs. For example, the older employed need CET to be able to keep up with changes in the work environment, whereas those who are retired from work increasingly seek CET for social purposes, personal growth and the development of meaningful leisure. In developing the CET indicator further, attention should be paid to the characteristics, learning needs and participation patterns of the different target and priority groups in the OECD countries.

This information would allow countries to clarify and guide decisions about the role of public policy involving CET as an intervention instrument.

### *Characteristics of the Providers*

In order to be able to develop indicators of the composition of the provision of CET, a first step is to distinguish participation by type of provider, using categories such as public vs. private; profit vs. non-profit; accredited vs. non-accredited; and credential vs. non-credential. The future indicators could show the roles which these respective providers play in adult continuing education and training.

### *Institutional Statistics*

The identification of the type of provider is also the first step in the development of indicators of costs, expenditures and the financing of CET. Future indicators on CET could show the amount of public and private money spent on CET, as well as comparisons of the costs of the various provisions. Whether these indicators could also be based on data collected from participating individuals, or whether they would need to be based on information gathered from the providers, is a further point to be worked on.

## 10. Conclusions

The main conclusion emerging from the above presentation is that a society which seeks to maximise both the individual and social rates of return to its investments in schooling and in continuing education and training, should look very carefully at the functions and roles of schooling, tertiary education, and continuing education and training, as the building blocks of the lifelong learning society.

International indicators on CET are needed to offer an insight into the different national situations and developments over the years.

# References

DOUGHERTY, C. (1992), "Evaluation of the economic and labor market effects of continuing education and training: practice and policy issues", in A.C. Tuijnman (Ed.), *Effectiveness Research into Continuing Education*, Pergamon Press, Oxford.

MINCER, J. (1989), "Human capital and the labour market. A review of current research", *Educational Researcher*, No. 18, pp. 27-34.

MINCER, J. (1991), "Job training: costs, returns, and wage profiles", in D. Stern and J.M.M. Ritzen (Eds.), *Market Failure in Training? New Economic Analysis and Evidence on Training of Adult Employees*, Springer-Verlag, Berlin.

Netherlands Ministry of Education and Science (1993), A *Lifetime of Learning: The Future Development of Adult Education*, Zoetermeer, Netherlands.

Netherlands Ministry of Social Affairs and Employment (1991), *Notitie scholing van werkenden* (Training for people in work), The Hague, Netherlands.

OECD (1991*a*), *Further Education and Training of the Labour Force in OECD Countries: Evidence and Issues,* Paris.

OECD (1991*b*), *Report on Training Statistics*, Paris.

OECD (1993), *Industry Training in Australia, Sweden and the United States,* Paris.

OECD (1994), *The OECD Jobs Study. Facts, Analysis, Strategies*, Paris.

OECD (1995), *Education at a Glance: OECD Indicators*, 3rd edition, CERI, Paris.

TUIJNMAN, A.C. (1987), *Monitoring Adult Education: Indicators for the Study of Equity in Swedish Adult Education,* Research report No. 80, Institute of International Education, Stockholm University, Stockholm.

TUIJNMAN, A.C. (1989), *Recurrent Education, Earnings, and Well-being: A 50-year Longitudinal Study of a Cohort of Swedish Men,* Acta Universitatis Stockholmiensis, Almqvist and Wiksell, Stockholm.

TUIJNMAN, A.C. (1993), "Paradigm shifts in adult education", in A.C. Tuijnman and M. van der Kamp (Eds.), *Learning across the Lifespan: Theories, Policies, Practices,* Pergamon Press, Oxford.

# Conclusions

*by*

***Bertil Bucht***
Ministry of Education and Science, Stockholm, Sweden

This chapter summarises the weaknesses, strengths and outcomes of the network's activities. One problem is that data availability often varies from one country to another, as does the quality of data. Another weakness is that the network has so far concentrated on formal school education. Hence, the recent work on a new indicator on continuing education and training for adults is something of a break-through. One of the strengths of the network is the great commitment by administrators, policy-makers and statisticians in all of the twenty participating countries. There is also a strength inherent in the network's theme, which brings ministries of education and ministries of labour together in a new and fruitful way. The chapter concludes by giving three options for the future programme of work for Network B: to go on as before, and to develop new indicators; to close down all network activities; or to adopt a "middle way", implying some continued developmental work, primarily on the three new indicators. Priority is given to the third of these alternatives.

As is evident from the preceding chapters, substantial progress has been made by Network B since 1990. This success is to no small extent due to the constructive contributions made by the representatives from twenty Member countries. Five "core" indicators were developed for the first edition of *Education at a Glance* (OECD, 1992) and have since then been refined. The latest issue of *Education at a Glance* (OECD, 1995) witnesses the birth of another three indicators of major relevance to policy-making – "Continuing Education and Training for Adults" (P08), "Educational Attainment of Workers" (R23) and "Labour Force Status for Leavers from Education" (R24).

A quite successful strategy in the process of developing new indicators has been to start by "casting the net widely". This was, for example, the case with the work on the new indicator, "Continuing Education and Training for Adults". Here, the network entered into a domain that is of particular relevance to policy-making in the OECD Member countries. There was a genuine interest in doing something in this very important field. The network had until then focused only on the formal education system. It was soon discovered, however, that adult education is a very diversified field with many differences in concepts, reference periods, and other technical aspects. But by deliberately pursuing some aspects and leaving others to be looked into at a later stage, the network got going and collected some data that would be used to draft a first version of our indicator on adult education and training. In a somewhat similar way, the network also agreed on the principle of never accepting ''the smallest common denominator'' of available data. This approach has brought with it challenges to those responsible for data collection in the various Member countries. But the advantage has been that the work could progress and that steps could be taken to promote data availability and data quality in some of the OECD countries.

*

* *

## Note de synthèse

*Ce dernier chapitre récapitule les lacunes, les points forts et les résultats des activités du Réseau B depuis quelques années. Une autre difficulté rencontrée aussi par les autres réseaux du projet INES est que les sources de données sont généralement limitées et varient d'un pays à l'autre. Un autre problème tient au fait que la qualité des données disponibles est souvent variable. Troisième point : certains indicateurs semblent présenter plus d'intérêt pour les décideurs que d'autres. Enfin, le Réseau B s'est concentré surtout sur le système d'enseignement formel. Jusqu'ici, il s'est peu intéressé à la formation continue des adultes. A cet égard, la mise au point d'un premier indicateur de la formation continue ouvre au Réseau B des perspectives nouvelles très intéressantes.*

*Parmi les atouts dont dispose le Réseau B, il convient de noter la participation active d'administrateurs, de responsables et de statisticiens dans les vingt pays Membres. Un autre avantage pour le réseau est la nature même de son activité – « Éducation et insertion professionnelle » – qui a souvent conduit les représentants des ministères de l'Éducation et des ministères du Travail à coopérer étroitement et de façon fructueuse.*

*En ce qui concerne les résultats concrets des travaux, il est à noter que le Réseau B a accompli des progrès notables depuis qu'il a commencé ses activités en 1990. Cinq indicateurs « de base » ont été publiés dans le premier numéro de* Regards sur l'éducation *(OCDE, 1992). Ceux-ci ont été affinés dans les éditions suivantes. La dernière édition de* Regards sur l'éducation *(OCDE, 1995) présente trois autres indicateurs très utiles pour les décideurs: la formation continue des adultes (P08), le niveau de formation des travailleurs (R23) et la situation au regard de l'emploi des personnes sorties du système scolaire (R24).*

*L'auteur conclut en proposant trois orientations pour le programme de travail futur du Réseau B. Premièrement, poursuivre dans la voie déjà tracée, c'est-à-dire mettre au point de nouveaux indicateurs pour tout le domaine considéré. Deuxièmement, mettre fin à toutes les activités du Réseau B. Troisièmement, choisir une solution « intermédiaire » qui consisterait à poursuivre certains travaux de mise au point axés essentiellement sur les trois nouveaux indicateurs. L'auteur privilégie la troisième option.*

\*

\* \*

## 1. Weaknesses and Strengths

Some obvious weaknesses have been noted throughout the network's history: data availability is often quite variable from one country to another, and the quality of data also varies. This problem is encountered also by the other networks engaged in the development of education indicators. Another weakness is that the focus has until very lately been only on formal school education, but the development of an indicator on continuing education and training for adults (P08) means that something of a break-through has been accomplished.

Among the strengths of the network, the first thing to be noted is perhaps the great commitment by administrators, policy-makers and statisticians in all of the twenty partic-ipating countries. There is also a strength inherent in the network's theme itself, which has brought ministries of education and ministries of labour together in a new and fruitful manner.

## 2. Options for the Future

With the General Assembly in Lahti in June 1995, the third phase of the INES project comes to an end. This will automatically affect the work programmes of the different networks, albeit in varying ways. As regards Network B, preparations have already been made to ensure that the database that has been built up at Statistics Sweden in the city of Örebro will be transferred to the OECD Secretariat in Paris. The intention is to create a capacity for continuing with regular data collection from the Secretariat in Paris, should this be recommended by the General Assembly and decided on by the OECD Education Committee and the CERI Governing Board.

At least three options could be envisaged for the future programme of work for Network B: 1) to go on as before, developing new indicators, with Sweden as the lead country and with no other changes than the transfer of the database to Paris; 2) to take the opposite action, *i.e.* to close down all network activities and to let the OECD in Paris go on with data collection on the five established ''core'' indicators and the three recently developed ones, all of them presented in the third edition of *Education at a Glance* (OECD, 1995); and 3) a middle way, implying continued developmental work, primarily on the three new indicators.

It is self-evident that the number of indicators in *Education at a Glance* cannot go on expanding in the way it has during these early years. Among other things, such an approach would be counterproductive, because it would make the overall picture too difficult to grasp. Today's gamut of some 50 to 55 indicators has already been called into question. There seems to be a general consensus on the need to halt the revisions and to consolidate the work as a whole. Thus, a simple continuation of the programme of work of Network B seems neither logical nor practicable.

On the other hand, judging by policy documents from both the OECD and many of its Member countries, there seems to be a sufficient and reliable consensus on the relevance to policy-making of the newly developed indicator of Network B, "Continuing Education and Training for Adults". This might suggest a need to go on, preferably in a small group of directly involved partners, with developmental work in order to refine this indicator and to make it even more useful to the OECD Member countries. The same approach could be applied to another recent innovation, the new indicator on "Rates of Return to Education". This indicator and the work that will be required to improve it are explained in Chapter 7 of this volume.

Such a "middle way" seems to be preferable to a sudden and total close-down of the work of an international group that has, in a short time, both achieved good results and pointed to possible directions for improving them.

Should the "middle way" be decided upon, an additional aspect is worth mentioning. Network B has not yet developed any indicator in which aspects of social background are explicitly taken into account. Several research reports in this field have, however, presented empirical data for certain countries. In one report, concerning Sweden and the United Kingdom, the authors identified three comparable and apparently crucial branching points in a typical educational career. Survival rates were calculated at each of these branching points for several cohorts of students. One of the findings of the report is that "clear class differences remain in the probabilities of surviving the two first branching points", but that "the extent of class inequality decreases at each subsequent branch". In the future, the INES project might take advantage of results from research projects on the influence of social class on people's choice of education and their performance in the labour market.

# ALSO AVAILABLE

**Education at a Glance - OECD Indicators**
                                    FF 220   FFE 285   £35   US$ 54   DM 83

**OECD Education Statistics, 1985-1992/Statistiques de l'enseignement de l'OCDE, 1985-1992** (bilingual)
                                    FF 160   FFE 210   £25   US$ 40   DM 60

**Measuring the Quality of Schools/Mesurer la qualité des établissements scolaires** (bilingual)
                                    FF 120   FFE 155   £20   US$ 29   DM 47

**Measuring What Students Learn/Mesurer les résultats scolaires** (bilingual)
                                    FF 110   FFE 140   £17   US$ 27   DM 40

**Public Expectations of the Final Stage of Compulsory Education/Le dernier cycle de l'enseignement obligatoire : quelle attente ?** (bilingual)
                                    FF 100   FFE 130   £16   US$ 25   DM 38

**Decision-Making Processes in the Education Systems of 14 OECD Countries** (forthcoming)

## ÉGALEMENT DISPONIBLES

**Regards sur l'éducation - Les indicateurs de l'OCDE**
FF 220   FFE 285   £35   US$ 54   DM 83

**OECD Education Statistics, 1985-1992/Statistiques de l'enseignement de l'OCDE, 1985-1992** (bilingue)
FF 160   FFE 210   £25   US$ 40   DM 60

**Measuring the Quality of Schools/Mesurer la qualité des établissements scolaires** (bilingue)
FF 120   FFE 155   £20   US$ 29   DM 47

**Measuring What Students Learn/Mesurer les résultats scolaires** (bilingue)
FF 110   FFE 140   £17   US$ 27   DM 40

**Public Expectations of the Final Stage of Compulsory Education/Le dernier cycle de l'enseignement obligatoire : quelle attente ?** (bilingue)
FF 100   FFE 130   £16   US$ 25   DM 38

**Les processus de décision dans 14 systèmes éducatifs de l'OCDE** (à paraître prochainement)

# MAIN SALES OUTLETS OF OECD PUBLICATIONS
# PRINCIPAUX POINTS DE VENTE DES PUBLICATIONS DE L'OCDE

**ARGENTINA – ARGENTINE**
Carlos Hirsch S.R.L.
Galería Güemes, Florida 165, 4° Piso
1333 Buenos Aires   Tel. (1) 331.1787 y 331.2391
Telefax: (1) 331.1787

**AUSTRALIA – AUSTRALIE**
D.A. Information Services
648 Whitehorse Road, P.O.B 163
Mitcham, Victoria 3132   Tel. (03) 873.4411
Telefax: (03) 873.5679

**AUSTRIA – AUTRICHE**
Gerold & Co.
Graben 31
Wien I   Tel. (0222) 533.50.14

**BELGIUM – BELGIQUE**
Jean De Lannoy
Avenue du Roi 202
B-1060 Bruxelles   Tel. (02) 538.51.69/538.08.41
Telefax: (02) 538.08.41

**CANADA**
Renouf Publishing Company Ltd.
1294 Algoma Road
Ottawa, ON K1B 3W8   Tel. (613) 741.4333
Telefax: (613) 741.5439
Stores:
61 Sparks Street
Ottawa, ON K1P 5R1   Tel. (613) 238.8985
211 Yonge Street
Toronto, ON M5B 1M4   Tel. (416) 363.3171
Telefax: (416)363.59.63
Les Éditions La Liberté Inc.
3020 Chemin Sainte-Foy
Sainte-Foy, PQ G1X 3V6   Tel. (418) 658.3763
Telefax: (418) 658.3763

Federal Publications Inc.
165 University Avenue, Suite 701
Toronto, ON M5H 3B8   Tel. (416) 860.1611
Telefax: (416) 860.1608
Les Publications Fédérales
1185 Université
Montréal, QC H3B 3A7   Tel. (514) 954.1633
Telefax : (514) 954.1635

**CHINA – CHINE**
China National Publications Import
Export Corporation (CNPIEC)
16 Gongti E. Road, Chaoyang District
P.O. Box 88 or 50
Beijing 100704 PR   Tel. (01) 506.6688
Telefax: (01) 506.3101

**CZECH REPUBLIC – RÉPUBLIQUE TCHÈQUE**
Artia Pegas Press Ltd.
Narodni Trida 25
POB 825
111 21 Praha 1   Tel. 26.65.68
Telefax: 26.20.81

**DENMARK – DANEMARK**
Munksgaard Book and Subscription Service
35, Nørre Søgade, P.O. Box 2148
DK-1016 København K   Tel. (33) 12.85.70
Telefax: (33) 12.93.87

**EGYPT – ÉGYPTE**
Middle East Observer
41 Sherif Street
Cairo   Tel. 392.6919
Telefax: 360-6804

**FINLAND – FINLANDE**
Akateeminen Kirjakauppa
Keskuskatu 1, P.O. Box 128
00100 Helsinki
Subscription Services/Agence d'abonnements :
P.O. Box 23
00371 Helsinki   Tel. (358 0) 12141
Telefax: (358 0) 121.4450

**FRANCE**
OECD/OCDE
Mail Orders/Commandes par correspondance:
2, rue André-Pascal
75775 Paris Cedex 16   Tel. (33-1) 45.24.82.00
Telefax: (33-1) 49.10.42.76
Telex: 640048 OCDE
Orders via Minitel, France only/
Commandes par Minitel, France exclusivement :
36 15 OCDE

OECD Bookshop/Librairie de l'OCDE :
33, rue Octave-Feuillet
75016 Paris   Tel. (33-1) 45.24.81.67
(33-1) 45.24.81.81
Documentation Française
29, quai Voltaire
75007 Paris   Tel. 40.15.70.00
Gibert Jeune (Droit-Économie)
6, place Saint-Michel
75006 Paris   Tel. 43.25.91.19
Librairie du Commerce International
10, avenue d'Iéna
75016 Paris   Tel. 40.73.34.60
Librairie Dunod
Université Paris-Dauphine
Place du Maréchal de Lattre de Tassigny
75016 Paris   Tel. (1) 44.05.40.13
Librairie Lavoisier
11, rue Lavoisier
75008 Paris   Tel. 42.65.39.95
Librairie L.G.D.J. - Montchrestien
20, rue Soufflot
75005 Paris   Tel. 46.33.89.85
Librairie des Sciences Politiques
30, rue Saint-Guillaume
75007 Paris   Tel. 45.48.36.02
P.U.F.
49, boulevard Saint-Michel
75005 Paris   Tel. 43.25.83.40
Librairie de l'Université
12a, rue Nazareth
13100 Aix-en-Provence   Tel. (16) 42.26.18.08
Documentation Française
165, rue Garibaldi
69003 Lyon   Tel. (16) 78.63.32.23
Librairie Decitre
29, place Bellecour
69002 Lyon   Tel. (16) 72.40.54.54

**GERMANY – ALLEMAGNE**
OECD Publications and Information Centre
August-Bebel-Allee 6
D-53175 Bonn   Tel. (0228) 959.120
Telefax: (0228) 959.12.17

**GREECE – GRÈCE**
Librairie Kauffmann
Mavrokordatou 9
106 78 Athens   Tel. (01) 32.55.321
Telefax: (01) 36.33.967

**HONG-KONG**
Swindon Book Co. Ltd.
13–15 Lock Road
Kowloon, Hong Kong   Tel. 2376.2062
Telefax: 2376.0685

**HUNGARY – HONGRIE**
Euro Info Service
Margitsziget, Európa Ház
1138 Budapest   Tel. (1) 111.62.16
Telefax : (1) 111.60.61

**ICELAND – ISLANDE**
Mál Mog Menning
Laugavegi 18, Pósthólf 392
121 Reykjavik   Tel. 162.35.23

**INDIA – INDE**
Oxford Book and Stationery Co.
Scindia House
New Delhi 110001   Tel.(11) 331.5896/5308
Telefax: (11) 332.5993
17 Park Street
Calcutta 700016   Tel. 240832

**INDONESIA – INDONÉSIE**
Pdii-Lipi
P.O. Box 4298
Jakarta 12042   Tel. (21) 573.34.67
Telefax: (21) 573.34.67

**IRELAND – IRLANDE**
Government Supplies Agency
Publications Section
4/5 Harcourt Road
Dublin 2   Tel. 661.31.11
Telefax: 478.06.45

**ISRAEL**
Praedicta
5 Shatner Street
P.O. Box 34030
Jerusalem 91430   Tel. (2) 52.84.90/1/2
Telefax: (2) 52.84.93
R.O.Y.
P.O. Box 13056
Tel Aviv 61130   Tél. (3) 49.61.08
Telefax (3) 544.60.39

**ITALY – ITALIE**
Libreria Commissionaria Sansoni
Via Duca di Calabria 1/1
50125 Firenze   Tel. (055) 64.54.15
Telefax: (055) 64.12.57
Via Bartolini 29
20155 Milano   Tel. (02) 36.50.83
Editrice e Libreria Herder
Piazza Montecitorio 120
00186 Roma   Tel. 679.46.28
Telefax: 678.47.51
Libreria Hoepli
Via Hoepli 5
20121 Milano   Tel. (02) 86.54.46
Telefax: (02) 805.28.86
Libreria Scientifica
Dott. Lucio de Biasio 'Aeiou'
Via Coronelli, 6
20146 Milano   Tel. (02) 48.95.45.52
Telefax: (02) 48.95.45.48

**JAPAN – JAPON**
OECD Publications and Information Centre
Landic Akasaka Building
2-3-4 Akasaka, Minato-ku
Tokyo 107   Tel. (81.3) 3586.2016
Telefax: (81.3) 3584.7929

**KOREA – CORÉE**
Kyobo Book Centre Co. Ltd.
P.O. Box 1658, Kwang Hwa Moon
Seoul   Tel. 730.78.91
Telefax: 735.00.30

**MALAYSIA – MALAISIE**
University of Malaya Bookshop
University of Malaya
P.O. Box 1127, Jalan Pantai Baru
59700 Kuala Lumpur
Malaysia   Tel. 756.5000/756.5425
Telefax: 756.3246

**MEXICO – MEXIQUE**
Revistas y Periodicos Internacionales S.A. de C.V.
Florencia 57 - 1004
Mexico, D.F. 06600   Tel. 207.81.00
Telefax : 208.39.79

**NETHERLANDS – PAYS-BAS**
SDU Uitgeverij Plantijnstraat
Externe Fondsen
Postbus 20014
2500 EA's-Gravenhage       Tel. (070) 37.89.880
Voor bestellingen:       Telefax: (070) 34.75.778

**NEW ZEALAND**
**NOUVELLE-ZÉLANDE**
Legislation Services
P.O. Box 12418
Thorndon, Wellington       Tel. (04) 496.5652
       Telefax: (04) 496.5698

**NORWAY – NORVÈGE**
Narvesen Info Center – NIC
Bertrand Narvesens vei 2
P.O. Box 6125 Etterstad
0602 Oslo 6       Tel. (022) 57.33.00
       Telefax: (022) 68.19.01

**PAKISTAN**
Mirza Book Agency
65 Shahrah Quaid-E-Azam
Lahore 54000       Tel. (42) 353.601
       Telefax: (42) 231.730

**PHILIPPINE – PHILIPPINES**
International Book Center
5th Floor, Filipinas Life Bldg.
Ayala Avenue
Metro Manila       Tel. 81.96.76
       Telex 23312 RHP PH

**PORTUGAL**
Livraria Portugal
Rua do Carmo 70-74
Apart. 2681
1200 Lisboa       Tel.: (01) 347.49.82/5
       Telefax: (01) 347.02.64

**SINGAPORE – SINGAPOUR**
Gower Asia Pacific Pte Ltd.
Golden Wheel Building
41, Kallang Pudding Road, No. 04-03
Singapore 1334       Tel. 741.5166
       Telefax: 742.9356

**SPAIN – ESPAGNE**
Mundi-Prensa Libros S.A.
Castelló 37, Apartado 1223
Madrid 28001       Tel. (91) 431.33.99
       Telefax: (91) 575.39.98

Libreria Internacional AEDOS
Consejo de Ciento 391
08009 – Barcelona       Tel. (93) 488.30.09
       Telefax: (93) 487.76.59
Llibreria de la Generalitat
Palau Moja
Rambla dels Estudis, 118
08002 – Barcelona
       (Subscripcions) Tel. (93) 318.80.12
       (Publicacions) Tel. (93) 302.67.23
       Telefax: (93) 412.18.54

**SRI LANKA**
Centre for Policy Research
c/o Colombo Agencies Ltd.
No. 300-304, Galle Road
Colombo 3       Tel. (1) 574240, 573551-2
       Telefax: (1) 575394, 510711

**SWEDEN – SUÈDE**
Fritzes Information Center
Box 16356
Regeringsgatan 12
106 47 Stockholm       Tel. (08) 690.90.90
       Telefax: (08) 20.50.21

Subscription Agency/Agence d'abonnements :
Wennergren-Williams Info AB
P.O. Box 1305
171 25 Solna       Tel. (08) 705.97.50
       Téléfax : (08) 27.00.71

**SWITZERLAND – SUISSE**
Maditec S.A. (Books and Periodicals - Livres
et périodiques)
Chemin des Palettes 4
Case postale 266
1020 Renens VD 1       Tel. (021) 635.08.65
       Telefax: (021) 635.07.80

Librairie Payot S.A.
4, place Pépinet
CP 3212
1002 Lausanne       Tel. (021) 341.33.47
       Telefax: (021) 341.33.45

Librairie Unilivres
6, rue de Candolle
1205 Genève       Tel. (022) 320.26.23
       Telefax: (022) 329.73.18

Subscription Agency/Agence d'abonnements :
Dynapresse Marketing S.A.
38 avenue Vibert
1227 Carouge       Tel.: (022) 308.07.89
       Telefax : (022) 308.07.99

See also – Voir aussi :
OECD Publications and Information Centre
August-Bebel-Allee 6
D-53175 Bonn (Germany)       Tel. (0228) 959.120
       Telefax: (0228) 959.12.17

**TAIWAN – FORMOSE**
Good Faith Worldwide Int'l. Co. Ltd.
9th Floor, No. 118, Sec. 2
Chung Hsiao E. Road
Taipei       Tel. (02) 391.7396/391.7397
       Telefax: (02) 394.9176

**THAILAND – THAÏLANDE**
Suksit Siam Co. Ltd.
113, 115 Fuang Nakhon Rd.
Opp. Wat Rajbopith
Bangkok 10200       Tel. (662) 225.9531/2
       Telefax: (662) 222.5188

**TURKEY – TURQUIE**
Kültür Yayinlari Is-Türk Ltd. Sti.
Atatürk Bulvari No. 191/Kat 13
Kavaklidere/Ankara       Tel. 428.11.40 Ext. 2458
Dolmabahce Cad. No. 29
Besiktas/Istanbul       Tel. 260.71.88
       Telex: 43482B

**UNITED KINGDOM – ROYAUME-UNI**
HMSO
Gen. enquiries       Tel. (071) 873 0011
Postal orders only:
P.O. Box 276, London SW8 5DT
Personal Callers HMSO Bookshop
49 High Holborn, London WC1V 6HB
       Telefax: (071) 873 8200
Branches at: Belfast, Birmingham, Bristol, Edin-
burgh, Manchester

**UNITED STATES – ÉTATS-UNIS**
OECD Publications and Information Centre
2001 L Street N.W., Suite 700
Washington, D.C. 20036-4910 Tel. (202) 785.6323
       Telefax: (202) 785.0350

**VENEZUELA**
Libreria del Este
Avda F. Miranda 52, Aptdo. 60337
Edificio Galipán
Caracas 106       Tel. 951.1705/951.2307/951.1297
       Telegram: Libreste Caracas

Subscription to OECD periodicals may also be
placed through main subscription agencies.

Les abonnements aux publications périodiques de
l'OCDE peuvent être souscrits auprès des
principales agences d'abonnement.

Orders and inquiries from countries where Distribu-
tors have not yet been appointed should be sent to:
OECD Publications Service, 2 rue André-Pascal,
75775 Paris Cedex 16, France.

Les commandes provenant de pays où l'OCDE n'a
pas encore désigné de distributeur peuvent être
adressées à : OCDE, Service des Publications,
2, rue André-Pascal, 75775 Paris Cedex 16, France.

1-1995

OECD PUBLICATIONS, 2 rue André-Pascal, 75775 PARIS CEDEX 16
PRINTED IN FRANCE
(91 95 05 3) ISBN 92-64-04357-8 - No. 47796 1995